W9-BYI-527

Table of Contents

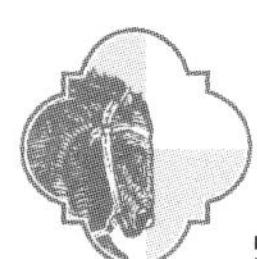

A Note to the Teacher

This is a book on traditional formal logic, a subject which a student might have studied in the Middle Ages. For the most part, the methodology of traditional logic was laid down by the ancient Greek philosopher Aristotle. It was taken up again, however, in the Middle Ages by the great doctors of the Church, and the formulations in this and the succeeding book, *Traditional Logic, Book II: Advanced Formal Logic*, are largely a result of their work.

The largest influence on this book comes from two other books: *Basic Logic*, by Raymond McCall, and *Introduction to Logic*, by Jacques Maritain. The examples are mostly mine.

The title of this book, *Traditional Logic: An Introduction to Formal Logic*, betrays a particular approach to the subject that I should say something about. First, this book discusses traditional logic rather than modern logic. Traditional logic is the study of the classical syllogism; modern logic is the study, primarily, of the calculus of propositions. You will not find truth tables in this book, nor will you find much of the mathematical formulations that are the common currency of modern logic. Despite a number of assumptions that traditional logicians find questionable, there is much in modern logic worthy of study. Traditional logic, however, seems to me to have a much more solid metaphysical foundation, as well as a closer relationship to ordinary human language. It is also a system unto itself which warrants separate study.

This book discusses traditional logic rather than modern logic. Traditional logic is the study of the classical syllogism; modern logic is the study, primarily, of the calculus of propositions.

Second, this book studies formal rather than informal logic. This can be seen most easily by the absence of a discussion of informal fallacies (although we do treat formal fallacies). The study of fallacies is often attempted because it seems to offer the teacher the best way to make the subject directly relevant, since they are easily understood and newspapers and magazines are filled with easily identifiable examples. But just because something has more immediate practical application does not mean that it is the best subject of study, or that it is the best to attempt first. Because a nice roof has more immediate appeal than a foundation does not mean that the foundation is less important, or that we should start on the roof first when building a house.

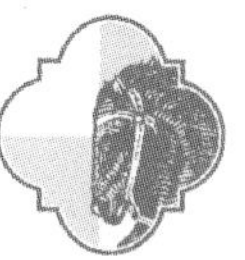

Because informal logic lacks a systematic structure, some of the benefits of rigorous logic instruction (such as an orderly habit of mind) are absent from its study. Like a house, a logical mind is best built upon a solid structure. A beginning study of formal logic provides this.

Traditional logic trains the mind to respect truth, and indeed assumes a Christian view of truth throughout, which is one of the reasons it appealed to the Medieval schoolmen. In fact, one of the reasons for including Chapters 1-3, abstract as they are, is precisely because they teach that there is such a thing as truth and that it can be comprehended (something you would think would be self-evident, but which we find ourselves defending against detractors much too often today).

This book has been prepared with homeschoolers in mind, although it is equally appropriate for private schools. It is the product of three years of logic instruction at Mars Hill, Lexington, a cooperative school for homeschooled children. Children met one day a week for classroom instruction (essentially the content presented in the following chapters), after which they completed the assignments in four-day installments at home.

Traditional logic trains the mind to respect truth, and indeed assumes a Christian view of truth throughout, which is one of the reasons it appealed to the Medieval schoolmen.

This book is best used with high school students, although I have used this material with 7th and 8th graders without any significant problems. Although Chapters 1-3 are the most abstract chapters of the book, I have found that they are among the most enjoyable to teach, and to learn—even for younger students. My own experience teaching students continues to indicate that these chapters are among my students' favorites. I don't pretend to know why this is. It might have something to do with the novelty of abstract thinking to students who have spent most of their academic lives dealing with matters more concrete; or it might be that students at this age simply appreciate dealing with deep philosophical ideas more than we give them credit for. These chapters can, however, be omitted or postponed if they are found to be too difficult.

This book is designed as a one-semester course, to be completed in approximately 15 weeks. However, my own experience, as well as feedback from several teachers, tells me that this book can be—and in most classroom situations should be—completed in less than a semester. This will allow extra time to spend on the more difficult material in *Book II*. Therefore, in such cases, I would recommend combining several pairs of chapters in *Book I*. The chapters I would recommend combining into a one-week lesson are as follows: Chapters 4 and 5; Chapters 6 and 7; and Chapters 12 and 13.

If there are suggestions about the text, I would be only too happy to hear them and would love to receive any comments you have. Simply write to Memoria Press.

Martin Cothran

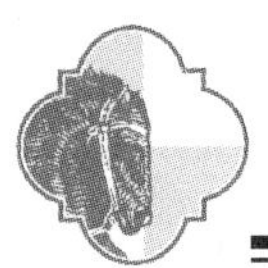

What is Logic?

Introduction. The best way to answer the question "What is logic?" is with a definition. But that is easier said than done. Throughout history, many people have thought and written about the subject of logic and many people have offered definitions. Some of them are useful and some are not.

Logic is the science of right thinking.

Josiah Royce, an American philosopher, defined logic as "the science of order," but this definition is so general that it really could include things outside of logic, and so it really doesn't tell us much.

Other definitions are a little too simple. The writer Oliver Wendell Holmes said, "Logic is logic. That's all I say." That obviously won't help us.

The writers of a book on fallacies (we'll explain what those are later) defined logic as "the defense against trickery." That's one thing logic is, but certainly not all.

Much better is the definition given by Raymond McCall: "Logic in general is the science of right thinking." Jacques Maritain, a very famous philosopher, had a similar definition. "Logic," he said, "is the art which enables us to proceed with order, ease, and correctness in the act of reason itself."

Irving Copi, who wrote a book on logic still used in many colleges, gets even a little more specific. "The distinction between correct and incorrect reasoning is the central problem with which logic deals." As you proceed in this book, you will see that this is so.

The History of Logic. The eighteenth-century German philosopher Immanuel Kant called Aristotle, the ancient Greek philosopher, the "father of logic." If we are thinking only of traditional, or ***formal***, logic (which is the only kind of logic we study in this book), this is true. In fact, formal logic has changed hardly at all since the time of Aristotle, who lived from 384-322 B.C.

Aristotle is considered the father of logic.

Shortly after the time of Aristotle, another Greek philosopher laid the groundwork for modern symbolic logic—his name was Chrysippus (279-206 B.C.). During the Middle Ages, the kind of logic developed by Chrysippus

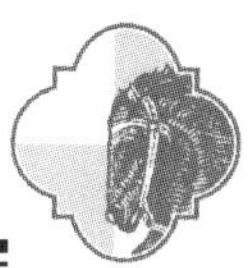

did not receive much attention. But in the 17th and early 18th centuries, philosophers began to take another look at the logical system of Chrysippus. One of the first and most famous of these is Gottfried Wilhelm Leibniz (1781-1848). Since then, many advances have been made in symbolic logic.

In addition, another form of logical thought, called ***induction***, has become a part of the subject that we know as logic. John Stuart Mill (1806-1873), who lived in the 19th century, pioneered the theories about induction that we study today.

The two main branches of logic are formal logic and material logic.

At the end of the 19th century and into our own, other logical methods have been developed, many of which have as much, if not more, to do with mathematics than with philosophy. Gottlob Frege (1848-1925), Alfred North Whitehead (1861-1947), and Bertrand Russell (1872-1970) are names associated with the more modern kinds of mathematical logic.

For our purposes, we will stick to the formal logic of Aristotle, which is just as useful today as it was when it was set forth over 2,300 years ago.

______ **The Two Main Branches of Logic.** There are two main branches of logic. One is called ***formal***, or "minor," logic, the other ***material***, or "major," logic. The two branches are quite distinct and deal with different problems.

Material logic is concerned with the *content* of argumentation. It deals with the *truth* of the terms and the propositions in an argument.

Formal logic is interested in the *form* or structure of reasoning. The truth of an argument is of only secondary consideration in this branch of logic. Formal logic is concerned with the method of deriving one truth from another.

The distinction between these two branches of logic was nicely described by G. K. Chesterton:

> Logic and truth ... have very little to do with each other. Logic is concerned merely with the fidelity and accuracy with which a certain process is performed, a process which can be performed with any materials, with any assumption. You can be as logical about griffins and basilisks as about sheep and pigs.... Logic, then, is not necessarily an instrument for finding out truth; on the contrary, truth is a necessary instrument for using logic—for using it, that is, for the discovery of further truth.... Briefly, you can only find truth with logic if you have already found truth without it.

Three important terms in logic are truth, validity, and soundness.

This last remark of Chesterton's is important. It is not the purpose of formal logic to discover truth. That is the business of everyday observation and, in certain more formal circumstances, empirical science. Logic serves only to lead us from one truth to another.

That is why, for example, you should not call a statement of fact ***logical*** or ***illogical*** (although this is commonly done in everyday argument). You should instead call it ***true*** or ***false***. Likewise, you should not call an argument (which contains several statements of fact) true or false. You should only call it ***valid*** or ***invalid***. Validity is the term we use when we mean to say that an argument is logical. The term ***soundness***, however, can be applied to an argument to say something about both its truth and its validity.

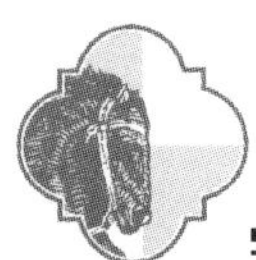

__________ **Truth, Validity, and Soundness.** ***Truth*** means the correspondence of a statement to reality. An argument is valid when its conclusion follows logically from its premises. The term 'soundness' is used to indicate that all the premises in an argument are true *and* that the argument is valid.

An argument can contain true premises and still be invalid. Likewise, it can be perfectly valid (or logical, if you prefer) and contain false premises. But if an argument is sound, its premises must be true and it must be valid.

If this sounds confusing, don't worry: these concepts will become clearer as we progress through the material in this book.

The verbal expression of a simple apprehension is called the *term*.

__________ **The Components of an Argument.** An argument contains several components. In order to illustrate what these components are and how they work in the reasoning process, let us begin with a simple argument:

All men are mortal
Socrates is a man
Therefore, Socrates is mortal

The first two statements are premises and the last is the conclusion. All arguments must have at least two premises and one conclusion.

On the face of it, this argument contains a number of words making up three statements which fit together into what looks and sounds like an argument. But there is more here than meets the eye.

In formal logic, we recognize three kinds of logical processes. We recognize that each of these originates in a ***mental act***, but that each also manifests itself as (and is known to us in the form of) a ***verbal expression***.

__________ **Term.** The mental act involved in the first of these three logical processes is called ***simple apprehension***. We call the verbal expression of simple apprehension the ***term***. A simple apprehension occurs when we first form in our mind a concept of something. When we put this concept into words, we have put this simple apprehension in the form of a term.

At the point of simple apprehension, we do not affirm or deny anything about it. We just possess or grasp it.

If in your mind, for example, you think of this book (the one you're reading right now), you are performing this first logical process. You are having a simple apprehension. And if you speak or write anything about it, you will have to use a term, the term 'book.'

In the argument above (the one about Socrates), there are three terms representing three simple apprehensions. The first is 'men'; the second is 'Socrates'; and the third is 'mortal.' Each one of these represents in our mind a concept that we have transformed into a word. The concept we call the ***simple apprehension*** and the word we call the ***term***.

Mental Act	Verbal Expression
Simple Apprehension	Term

The verbal expression of a judgment is called a *proposition*.

__________ **Proposition.** The mental act involved in the second of these three logical processes is called ***judgment***. The verbal expression of a judgment is called a ***proposition***. We perform a judgment any time we think in our mind that something *is* something else (which we call affirmation), and also when we think that something *is not* something else (which we call denial). To judge is to affirm or deny.

If you think that this book is boring, then you are performing a judgment. If you verbally express this judgment, you will have to do it in the form of a proposition, the proposition "This book is boring." The judgment is the mental act you have when you think that this book is boring, and the proposition is the statement you make to express that thought.

In the argument above, there are three propositions expressed. The first is "All men are mortal"; the second is "Socrates is a man"; and the third is "Socrates is mortal." Each one of these represents in our mind a thought that something is something else: that all 'men' are 'mortal'; that 'Socrates' is a 'man'; and that 'Socrates' is 'mortal.'

We should point out that some people use the word 'statement' instead of 'proposition.' They mean the same thing, but to be consistent, we will use the word 'proposition.'

Mental Act	Verbal Expression
Judgment	Proposition

The verbal expression of a deductive inference is called a *syllogism*.

__________ **Syllogism.** The mental act involved in the third of these three logical processes is called ***deductive inference***. We call the verbal expression of deductive inference the ***syllogism***. A deductive inference occurs when we make the logical connections in our mind between the terms in the argument in a way that shows us that the conclusion either follows or does not follow from the premises. When we verbally express this in an argument, we have put this deductive inference in the form of a syllogism.

It is at this point that we are said to make progress in knowledge. It is through the process of deductive inference, as expressed in a syllogism, that we can say, as we explained above, that we have gone from one truth or set of truths to another truth.

Let's say the reason you think this book is boring is because you think all books are boring. If this were true, you would be performing a deductive inference. You would be thinking to yourself, all books are boring, and this is a book. Therefore, this book is boring. And if you verbally expressed this deductive inference, you would do it in the form of a syllogism. The judgment expressed by "All books are boring" and "This is a book" are different than the judgment "This book is boring." Through deductive inference, however, you can go from these first two to the last one. In this way, you have gone from one set of truths to another truth (if indeed they are true, which hopefully they are not).

We would say that the argument above (the one about Socrates), in its entirety, is a syllogism. It expresses a deductive inference that logically connects certain simple apprehensions that are parts of three judgments. And this process has been expressed in the form of a syllogism.

Mental Act	Verbal Expression
Deductive Inference	Syllogism

If we now put this all together, keeping our distinction between mental acts and verbal expressions, it would look like this:

Mental Act	Verbal Expression
Simple Apprehension	Term
Judgment	Proposition
Deductive Inference	Syllogism

In order to give ourselves a mental picture of these three logical processes, let us think of a man walking. In order to get from, say, one room to another, he has to pick up his foot and take several steps in order to get to the room that is his destination. The initial act—picking up his foot—is like the initial logical act of simple apprehension. Taking a full step is like making a judgment. And stringing all the steps together into one movement is like deductive inference—we move from one place to another.

The initial act—picking up his foot—is like the initial logical act of simple apprehension. Taking a full step is like making a judgment. And stringing all the steps together into one movement is like deductive inference.

Summary. We started out by defining logic as "the science of right thinking." We said there are two main branches of logic. One is called ***formal***, or ***minor***, logic, the other ***material***, or ***major***, logic. Material logic is concerned with the *content* of argumentation. Formal logic is interested in the *form* or structure of reasoning. We defined ***truth*** as correspondence with reality. We said an argument is ***valid*** when its conclusion follows logically from its premises. And we said that ***soundness*** indicates that all the premises in an argument are true *and* that the argument is valid.

We said also that all arguments must contain two premises and a conclusion. And we said, finally, that there are three mental acts that make up the logical process: ***simple apprehension***, ***judgment***, and ***deductive inference***. These three mental acts correspond to three verbal expressions: ***term***, ***proposition***, and ***syllogism***.

______________**Exercises for Day 1.** **Read the entire chapter. You may read it fairly quickly on this first reading. Don't expect to understand everything you read. Try only to get a general idea of what the chapter is about. Next, read the beginning sections of the introduction: "The History of Logic" and "The Two Main Branches of Logic." Read these sections carefully and try to fully understand them.**

1. Based on what you have read in this chapter, what is the definition of logic?

2. Who was called the "father of logic"?

3. Who laid the groundwork for modern symbolic logic?

4. Give the name of one philosopher who made advances in symbolic logic.

5. Who pioneered the theories about induction that we study today?

6. Give the names of three people whose names are associated with modern kinds of mathematical logic.

7. Give the names of the two main branches of logic.

8. Explain the first of the main branches of logic (in Question 7) and describe it in your own words.

9. Explain the second of the main branches of logic (in Question 7) and describe it in your own words.

10. Indicate whether the following statements are true or false:

T F The purpose of formal logic is to discover truth.
T F It is necessary to have logic in order to discover truth.
T F Logic leads us from one truth to another.
T F A statement can be true or false.
T F A statement can be valid or invalid.
T F An argument can be true or false.
T F An argument can be valid or invalid.
T F Truth is only of secondary consideration in formal logic.

______________**Exercises for Day 2.** **Read "Truth, Validity, and Soundness" and "The Components of an Argument." Read them carefully.**

11. On the basis of today's reading, define 'truth.'

12. On the basis of today's reading, explain what it means to say an argument is valid.

13. On the basis of today's reading, define 'soundness.'

14. Indicate whether the following statements are true or false:

T F An argument can contain true premises and be invalid.
T F An argument can be sound and contain false premises.
T F A sound argument must be valid.
T F A valid argument must be sound.
T F An argument with true premises can be unsound.
T F An argument can contain only one premise.

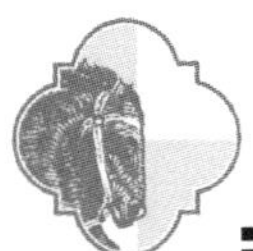

15. In the following argument, identify the premises and the conclusion by writing the words 'premise' or 'conclusion' in the space next to the statement.

All men are mortal
Socrates is a man
Therefore, Socrates is mortal

16. Name the three types of logical processes (or acts of the mind) involved in logic.

__________ Exercises for Day 3. **Read "Term" and "Proposition."**

17. Each of these logical processes or mental acts (in Question 16 above) originates in a ______________ ___________ and manifests itself in the form of a _________________________________ .

18. What is the mental act involved in the first of the three kinds of logical processes?

19. What is the verbal expression connected to this mental act (in Question 18)?

20. What occurs in our minds when we have a simple apprehension?

21. If you think of this book and have the concept in your mind, you are having a simple apprehension. What is the term you use to verbally express this particular simple apprehension?

22. Name the terms included in the argument in Question 15 above.

23. What does each one of these terms (in Question 22) represent?

24. What is the mental act involved in the second of the three kinds of logical processes?

25. What is the verbal expression connected to this mental act (in Question 24)?

26. What occurs in our minds when we perform a judgment?

27. If you think that this book is boring by affirming in your mind that this is so, your mind is performing a judgment. What is the term you use to verbally express this judgment?

28. Indicate the propositions included in the argument in Question 15 above.

29. What does each one of these propositions (in Question 28) represent?

__________ Exercises for Day 4. **Read "Syllogism" and "Summary." Read them carefully.**

30. What is the mental act involved in the third of the three kinds of logical processes?

31. What is the verbal expression connected to this mental act (in Question 30)?

32. Describe in no less than one and no more than three sentences what occurs in our minds when we engage in deductive inference.

33. If you think that because all books are boring and that this is a book, and that therefore this book is boring, your mind engaged in deductive inference. What is the term you use to verbally express this deductive inference?

34. Fill out the chart below, listing the mental acts and their corresponding verbal expressions in the order in which we have covered them:

Mental Act	Verbal Expression
■ ________________	■ ________________
■ ________________	■ ________________
■ ________________	■ ________________

35. Draw a line to indicate which action best describes what each mental act is like:

Taking a step	Simple Apprehension
Picking up your foot	Deductive Inference
Walking from one place to another	Judgment

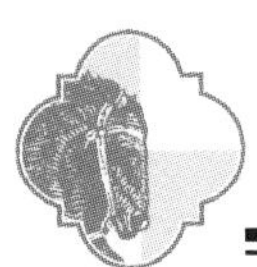

What is Simple Apprehension?

Introduction. In this chapter, we will discuss the first of the three parts of logic, simple apprehension. We will do this by defining what simple apprehension is. Let us try to explain simple apprehension by an illustration. Let's say we have a simple apprehension of a chair. What happens in our minds when we have a simple apprehension of a chair?

Generally speaking, three things happen. First, we perceive it with our senses; second, we form an image of it in our minds; and, thirdly, we conceive its meaning. Although all three of these things occur when we have a sense perception, it is this final act, the conception of meaning, that we properly speak of as simple apprehension.

Three things generally occur during simple apprehension: we perceive it with our senses, we have a mental image of it, and we conceive the meaning of it.

What is Sense Perception? Let's use an illustration to try to understand sense perception. When you look at a chair, when your senses (in this case your sight) present a chair to your mind, you have a sense perception. In other words, your senses perceive the chair. This sense perception is present when you are looking at the chair, but goes away when you stop looking at the chair. You will continue to have a sense perception of the chair as long as you look at it. But when you stop looking at the chair, your sense perception ceases.

The sense perception of the chair is different from the chair itself, since the sense perception occurs in your mind, while the chair exists outside of your mind. The sense perception lasts as long as you see or hear or smell or taste or touch an object and stops when you stop doing these things.

Sense perception is the act of seeing or hearing or smelling or tasting or touching.

What is a Mental Image? When you have a sense perception of something—when you see or hear or smell or taste or touch an object—an image forms in your mind. When you see a chair, for example, an image—which has color and shape—forms as a result of the sense perception you have of the chair. When the sense perception ceases, however—when, for example, you stop looking at the chair—the image can continue. And this image will

occur again in your mind whenever you think about the chair—even if you are not looking at the chair.

This happens, for example, every time you remember something you have seen before.

Like the sense perception you had when you looked at the chair, this mental image of the chair is different from the chair itself, since the chair exists outside the mind, while the mental image exists inside the mind only. Furthermore, this mental image of the chair is different from the sense perception because, while the sense perception lasts only as long as you are looking at the chair, the mental image can be present even when you are not perceiving the chair through your senses.

In short, the mental image is different from the chair, and the mental image is also different from the sense perception.

A mental image is the image of an object formed in the mind as a result of a sense perception of that object.

Simple apprehension is an act by which the mind grasps the concept or general meaning of an object without affirming or denying anything about it.

__________ **What is a Concept?** The third aspect of simple apprehension is idea or ***concept***. When you look at a chair, there is something else that happens in your mind other than a sense perception and a mental image. It is the idea or concept of the chair. When you grasp the concept of something, like a chair, you understand what a chair is. That is all we mean by 'concept.'

Although the idea of a chair in your mind may be accompanied by the sense perception of a chair or by the mental image of a chair, it does not have to be. You can have the concept without the sense perception and without the mental image.

For example, you may be reading this book right now but not have a chair around to look at, and yet you can still understand what is meant by the word 'chair.' In other words, you don't have to look at a chair to understand what a chair is. Similarly, you may be reading this book right now and not even have a mental image of chair and still understand what the word 'chair' means. You may understand what a chair is without having a picture of a chair in your mind.

Understanding what we mean when we talk about a concept is important in understanding what we mean when we talk about simple apprehension, since simple apprehension is the grasping of a concept. Remember also that simply apprehending, or understanding, something is different from making a judgment about it. Simple apprehension takes place prior to making a judgment. (We will talk about judgment in later chapters.)

Simple apprehension is an act by which the mind grasps the concept or general meaning of an object without affirming or denying anything about it.

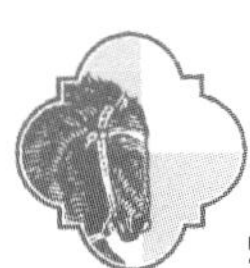

____________ **Concept vs. Image.** While a mental image is representative of something tangible and material (for example, it has shape and color), the simple apprehension is the grasp of something intangible and immaterial. A simple apprehension itself does not have shape or color; it is the act of understanding a universal meaning.

When we have a simple apprehension of something—when, in other words, we understand it—we do not just get a glimpse of the sensible qualities of it, like its color and shape; we grasp the ***essence*** (or meaning) of the thing.

This becomes clearer when we consider terms like 'man' (meaning 'human being'). When we think of the concept 'man,' we may have some kind of image in our minds, such as an actual man, tall, with blond hair, blue eyes, and light skin. But when someone else thinks of the concept 'man,' he may have a completely different image in his mind. He may think of an actual man who is short, with dark hair, brown eyes, and dark skin. Although the mental images we have when we think of the concept 'man' are completely different, that doesn't mean that we do not both understand the same concept 'man.' We may have exactly the same understanding of what 'man' is, yet have very different mental images that we associate with it.

The process by which a simple apprehension is derived from a sense perception and a mental image is called *abstraction*.

____________ **Abstraction.** The process by which a simple apprehension is derived from a sense perception and mental image is called ***abstraction***. Through abstraction, an object such as a chair is lifted from the level of the senses to the level of the intellect.

____________ **Simple Apprehension vs. Judgment.** If we affirm or deny anything about a simple apprehension of the chair, we are going beyond simple apprehension—the first aspect of logic—and engaging in judgment—the second aspect of logic. If, in other words, we think, "The chair is brown," then we are going beyond simple apprehension to affirm something about the chair and engaging in judgment. If, however, we think simply 'chair,' merely have an idea of a chair, then we are engaging in simple apprehension.

____________ **Summary.** In this chapter, we have discussed the meaning of simple apprehension. We said three things generally occur during the process of simple apprehension: we perceive it with our senses, we have a mental image of it, and we conceive the meaning of it. Note that the term 'simple apprehension' is used both to refer to the act of conceptualizing something as well as the entire process leading up to that act. We said, finally, that the process by which a simple apprehension is derived from a sense perception and a mental image is called ***abstraction***.

Exercises for Day 1. **Read the entire chapter. You may read it fairly quickly on this first reading. Try only to get a general idea of what the chapter is about. Read the beginning sections of Chapter 1: "What is Simple Apprehension?" and "What is Sense Perception?" Read these sections carefully and try to understand them as best you can.**

1. What are the three things associated with simple apprehension?

2. Which one of the three parts of the answer to Question 1 is the simple apprehension itself?

3. Which two of the three answers in Question 1 are connected with simple apprehension, but are not simple apprehension itself?

4. Which one of the three things associated with simple apprehension (in Question 1) is present when we are looking at something with our eyes, but ceases once we are no longer looking at it?

5. Why is the sense perception of a chair different from the chair itself?

6. What is the definition of 'sense perception'?

Exercises for Day 2. **Read "What is a Mental Image?" Read it carefully.**

7. What happens in your mind when you have a sense perception?

8. When you remember something you have seen, say, a chair, are you having a sense perception or a mental image?

9. Give one reason why a mental image of a chair must be different from the sense perception of the chair.

10. What is the definition of 'mental image'?

Read "What is a Concept?"

11. What are you having when you understand the meaning of the concept 'chair'?

12. Is the simple apprehension you experience when you understand the meaning of an object, such as a chair, the same as or different from the sense perception you experience when looking at a chair or the mental image in your mind that results from the sense perception?

13. Give one reason why a mental image must be different from simple apprehension itself.

14. What is the definition of 'simple apprehension'?

15. What is another term used for simple apprehension?

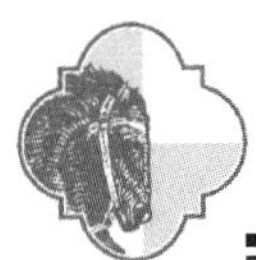

_________ Exercises for Day 3. **Read "Concept vs. Image." Read it carefully.**

16. What do we grasp when we have a simple apprehension of a thing?

17. If you have a mental image in your mind when you think of the concept 'man' and someone else has a different mental image, does that mean you are each thinking of a different concept? Explain, using the concept 'man.'

18. Offer an explanation for your answer in Question 17 above, only this time use an example other than that of 'man.'

Read "Abstraction."

19. What is the definition of the term 'abstraction'?

_________ Exercises for Day 4. **Read "Simple Apprehension vs. Judgment."**

20. Explain at what point you go from simple apprehension to judgment.

21. Indicate whether the following statements are true or false:

T F Mental image is the simple apprehension itself.

T F A sense perception of something we see disappears when we are no longer looking at it.

T F A sense perception of a chair is different from the chair itself because the chair exists in the mind while the sense perception exists outside the mind.

T F Sense perception is the act of seeing or hearing or smelling or tasting or touching.

T F When we see something, an image forms in our mind, which we call a 'mental image.'

T F A sense perception lasts only as long as we are perceiving the object through our senses.

T F A mental image is the image of an object formed in our mind as a result of a sense perception of that object.

T F The idea of a chair in your mind must be accompanied by the sense perception of a chair or by the mental image of a chair.

T F Simple apprehension is an act by which the mind grasps the concept or general meaning of an object and affirms or denies something about it.

T F The terms 'concept' and 'simple apprehension' mean the same thing.

T F A simple apprehension (or concept) has shape and color.

T F When we have a simple apprehension of a thing, we grasp the thing's essence.

T F If you have a different mental image of a concept than another person has, then you both cannot be thinking of the same concept.

T F The process by which a simple apprehension is derived from a sense perception and mental image is called 'abstraction.'

T F If we were to affirm or deny something about a concept, we would be going beyond simple apprehension to judgment.

_________ Review Exercises.

22. What is the definition of 'logic'?

23. On the basis of last week's reading, define 'truth.'

24. Name the three types of logical processes (or acts of the mind) involved in logic.

25. Fill out the chart below, listing the mental acts and their corresponding verbal expressions in the order in which we have covered them:

Mental Act	Verbal Expression
■ ____________________	■ ____________________
■ ____________________	■ ____________________
■ ____________________	■ ____________________

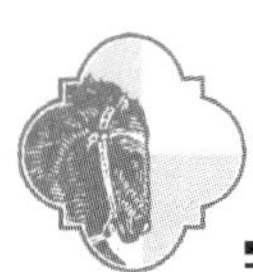

Comprehension and Extension

Introduction. In the last chapter we explained what simple apprehension was. We said that it was an act by which the mind grasped the essence or meaning of a thing without affirming or denying anything about it. We explained how simple apprehension differed from sense perception and image, and that simple apprehension is different from judgment because simple apprehension does not affirm or deny anything about a concept, while judgment does.

In this chapter, we will discuss not the *definition* of simple apprehension (since we have already done that), but the *properties* of simple apprehension. The definition of something is an explanation of what it is. The properties of something are the things that distinguish it and help us to know how it differs from other things.

The two properties of simple apprehension are ***comprehension*** and ***extension***.

The two properties of simple apprehension are *comprehension* and *extension*.

Comprehension. Some concepts (and remember, 'concept' is just another word for simple apprehension) are simple, but some are complex.

In the last chapter, the example we used when we talked about simple apprehension was a chair. When we are asked what a chair is, we can simply say, "A structure of metal or wood designed for people to sit in." The concept of a chair is a fairly simple concept. But there are other concepts that are not so simple. For example, the concept 'man' is not a simple concept. It is not a simple thing to say exactly what a man (meaning 'human being') is.

The ancient Greek philosopher Plato once gave a tongue-in-cheek definition of 'man.' He said a man was a "featherless biped." Technically speaking, Plato's definition is correct. Human beings don't have feathers and they are all bipeds (animals that walk around on two feet). But if you were an intelligent being (say, from another planet) who had never seen a human being before, would this description really tell you enough to know what a man is? It certainly counts out birds, since they have feathers. And it counts out horses, because they walk around on four legs instead of two. But even if the term "featherless biped" applied only to human beings, it still wouldn't tell us what a man is.

The expression "featherless biped" doesn't tell us that he is rational, or that he is the only being that is created in the image of God. It doesn't tell us many things about human beings that make up their nature or essence.

But there is a way to break down the complex elements of a concept. These elements of complex meaning are made clear by the use of the idea of comprehension.

Comprehension can be defined as ***the completely articulated sum of the intelligible aspects, or elements (or notes) represented by a concept***.

All this means is that when we ask what a man is, we are asking, "What is the comprehension of the concept 'man'?"

When we ask the question "What is man?" we can correctly say, as did Plato (in a more serious moment), that a man is a 'rational animal.' We know (or at least we should know) what the term 'rational' means. To be rational is simply to have the ability to distinguish the true from the false.

C*omprehension* can be defined as the completely articulated sum of the intelligible aspects or elements (or *notes*) represented by a concept.

The term 'rational' is a simple concept, which doesn't mean that it is easy to understand, only that it cannot be broken down into simpler parts. But the term 'animal' is not simple, since it can be broken down into simpler parts. So when we try to answer the question "What is an animal?" we continue to break it down into simpler and simpler concepts until we have included all the simple concepts that make up the concept 'animal.'

In fact, we can break down the concept 'animal' into the following simple concepts:

- ✔ sentient
- ✔ living
- ✔ material
- ✔ substance

The word 'sentient' means it has senses, such as sight, hearing, etc. The word 'material' means it has a body, rather than being purely spiritual—like angels. The word 'substance' simply means it is something rather than nothing.

Notes. In logic, each one of these simple concepts we used above to define the complex concept 'animal' (sentient, living, etc.) are called ***notes*** (look back at the definition of comprehension we used above). As you can see, there are four simple concepts into which we have broken the complex concept 'animal.' Therefore, the concept 'animal' is said to have four notes. In other words, the answer to the question "What is an animal?" is "A sentient, living, material substance."

If, on the other hand, we go back to the term 'man,' which we said was a rational animal, and ask, "What is a man?" we say, "A rational, sentient, living, material substance." The concept 'animal,' in other words, has four notes:

- ✔ sentient
- ✔ living
- ✔ material
- ✔ substance

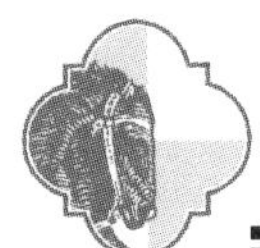

The concept 'man,' on the other hand, has five notes:

- rational
- sentient
- living
- material
- substance

__________ **The Porphyrian Tree.** When you were very young you may have played a game called "Animal, vegetable, mineral." In it, a thing was presented to you and you were to tell whether the thing was an animal, a vegetable, or a mineral. The use of the term 'comprehension,' in which we state the notes (or categories) to which a thing belongs, is a little bit like this childhood game—it is just more complex.

We can put all the notes by which we comprehend an object into a diagram. The diagram you see in Figure 2-1 is called the ***Porphyrian Tree*** because it was invented by the third-century logician Porphyry. It gives us a convenient way to break down a complex concept into the simple concepts out of which it is made.

We can apply comprehension to any object. In fact, let's apply it to the concept 'chair,' since that is the concept we used in the last chapter.

Notice that the first category on the Porphyrian Tree is ***substance***. If a thing is a thing at all—in other words, if it exists—then it is said to have substance. A unicorn, for example, could not be said to have substance because there are no unicorns—they don't exist. But a chair exists, so it must therefore have substance. But what kind of substance?

Is it material substance or nonmaterial (or spiritual) substance? A chair is, of course, a material substance; in other words, it has ***body*** (the next level of the Porphyrian Tree). Now we know, then, that a chair is ***material substance***. But what kind of material substance? Is it living material substance or non-living material substance? A chair (let's say it is a metal chair instead of a wooden one) is a non-living material substance, since metal cannot be said to be living.

And that is about as much as we can say about it. We can say, then, that the complex concept 'chair' consists of the following simple concepts:

- material
- substance

In other words, we could go only two steps down on the Porphyrian Tree, and therefore the concept 'chair' has only two notes. It is a substance with a body. The answer to the question "What is a chair?" then, is "A non-living, material substance." [Notice here that there are three adjectives we use to describe the chair. This would make you think that the concept 'chair' has three notes. But the term 'non-living' is there to let you know that it doesn't go down to the next step on the Porphyrian Tree. The term 'non-living' is sort of like a logical cul-de-sac that doesn't go anywhere. On the Porphyrian Tree, only one of the two ways at each step leads to the next step down (the ones that go to the left). The other leads nowhere. If we had determined that the chair was living, rather than non-living, we could have gone down one more step on the Porphyrian Tree and it would have had three notes. But it is not living, so it has only two.]

To ask what is the comprehension of a concept, then, is to ask the question "What is a man (or animal or chair, etc.)?"

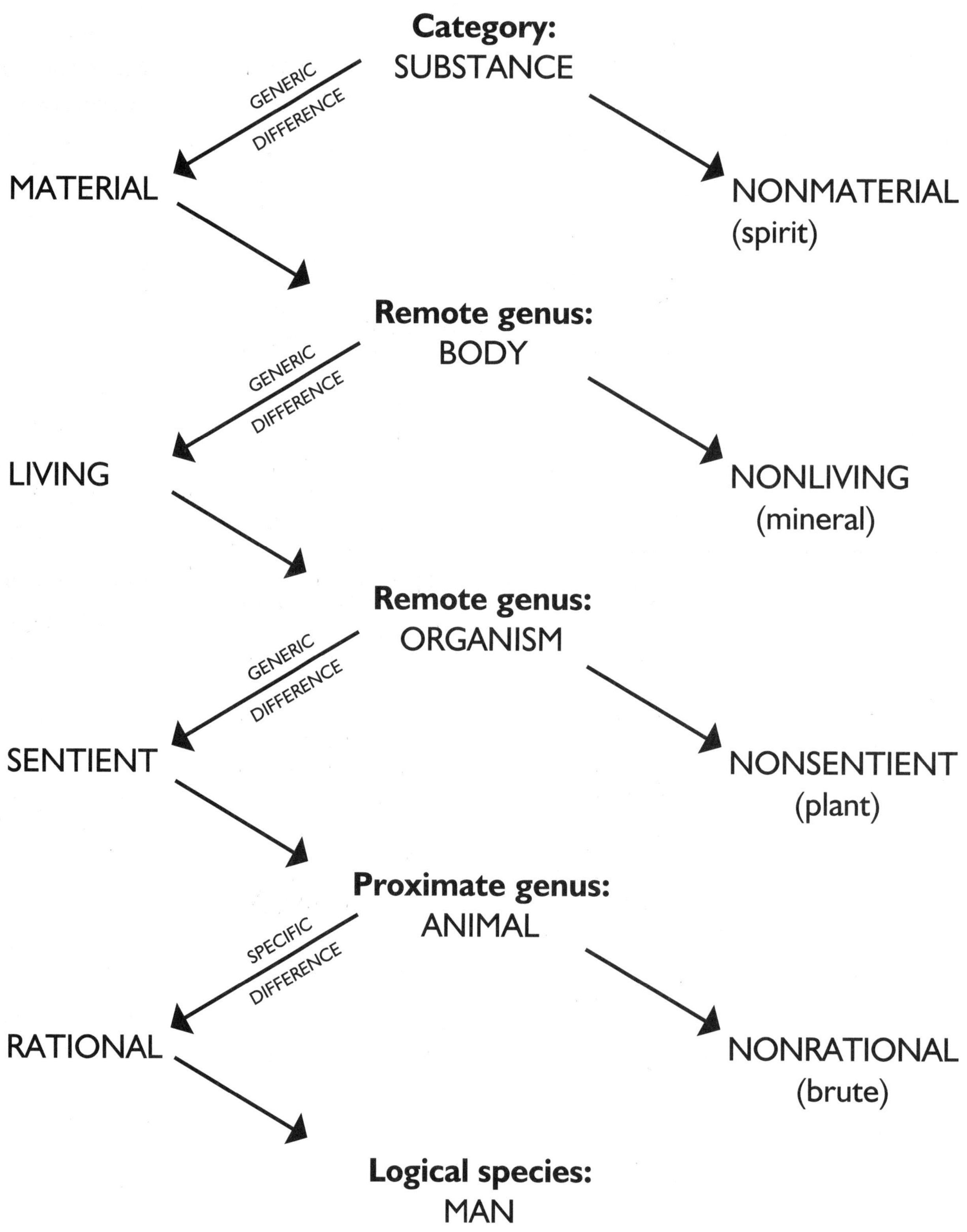
The Porphyrian Tree
Category:
SUBSTANCE
GENERIC
DIFFERENCE
MATERIAL
NONMATERIAL
(spirit)
Remote genus:
BODY
GENERIC
DIFFERENCE
LIVING
NONLIVING
(mineral)
Remote genus:
ORGANISM
GENERIC
DIFFERENCE
SENTIENT
NONSENTIENT
(plant)
Proximate genus:
ANIMAL
SPECIFIC
DIFFERENCE
RATIONAL
NONRATIONAL
(brute)
Logical species:
MAN

Figure 2-1

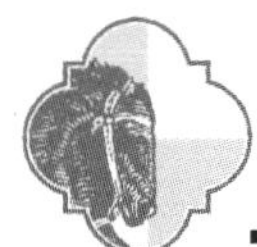

To ask what is the comprehension of a concept, then, is to ask the question "What is a man (or animal or chair, etc.)?"

You can see that the concept 'animal,' which we defined as a substance that was material, living, and sentient, is on the fourth step down on the Tree, indicating it has four notes. The concept 'man,' on the other hand, is five steps down, indicating it has five notes.

To ask what is the extension of a concept is to ask, "To what does the concept *man* refer?"

__________ **Extension.** The second of the two properties of simple apprehension we study in this chapter is the property of ***extension***.

To ask about the extension of a concept is not to ask, "What is a man (animal, chair, etc.)?" but it is to ask instead, "To what does the concept 'man' refer?"

For example, the answer to the question "What is man?" (comprehension) is "A substance that is material, living, sentient, and rational." But the answer to the question "What is the extension of man?" is "All the men who have ever lived, who are now living, and who will live in the future."

We can ask the same questions about the concept 'animal.' The answer to the question "What is an animal?" is "A substance that is material, living, and sentient." And the answer to the question "What is the extension of animal?" is "All the animals (including men, lions, dogs, fish, insects, etc.) that have ever lived, are now living, and that ever will live."

Comprehension tells us what the essence of a thing is; extension tells us the things to which that essence applies.

The greater the comprehension a concept has, the less extension it has; and the more extension it has, the less comprehension.

__________ **The Relationship between Comprehension and Extension.** Notice an important thing about the relationship between comprehension and extension; namely, the greater number of notes a concept has, the less extension it has. The concept 'man' has five notes—one more than the concept 'animal.' Yet, while the concept 'animal' has only four notes, the variety of things to which the concept 'animal' applies is much greater.

In other words, while the concept 'man' has more notes (five) than the concept 'animal' (four), the concept 'man' applies to fewer things. While the comprehension of the concept 'man' is greater than the concept 'animal,' the extension of the concept 'animal' is greater than the concept 'man.'

The greater the comprehension a concept has, the less extension it has; and the more extension it has, the less comprehension.

__________ **Summary.** In this chapter, we have discussed the properties of simple apprehension. We said there are two properties of simple apprehension: ***comprehension*** and ***extension***. The comprehension of a simple apprehension is a description of what a concept is. The extension of a concept is a description of the things to which a concept applies. We said, finally, that the greater the comprehension of a concept, the less its extension; and the greater its extension, the less its comprehension.

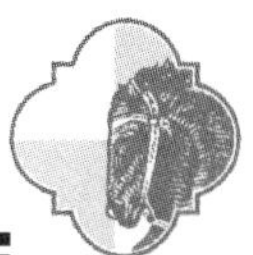

_______ **Exercises for Day 1.** **Read the entire chapter. Try only to get a general idea of what the chapter is about. Then read the introduction. Read this section carefully and try to understand it as best you can.**

1. What are we discussing in this chapter?

2. What are the two properties of simple apprehension?

Read "Comprehension." Read it carefully.

3. Is the concept 'man' simple or complex?

4. Is the concept 'chair' simple or complex?

5. What was the philosopher Plato's tongue-in-cheek definition of 'man'?

6. Was Plato's definition correct, technically speaking?

7. What is the problem with Plato's definition?

8. What is the definition of 'comprehension'?

9. Define the following terms: 'sentient,' 'material,' and 'substance.'

_______ **Exercises for Day 2.** **Read "Notes." Read it carefully.**

10. What are the simple concepts we use to define a complex concept called?

11. How many notes does the concept 'animal' have?

12. Using the idea of comprehension, what is the answer to the question "What is an animal?"

13. How many notes does the concept 'man' have?

14. Using the idea of comprehension, what is the answer to the question "What is a man?"

Read "The Porphyrian Tree." Read it carefully.

15. What is the diagram invented by the third-century logician Porphyry called?

16. What does Porphyry's invention help us do?

17. Using the Porphyrian Tree, explain how you find the number of notes in the concept 'chair.'

18. Using the Porphyrian Tree, explain how you find the number of notes in the concept 'animal.'

19. Using the Porphyrian Tree, explain how you find the number of notes in the concept 'man.'

_________ Exercises for Day 3. Read "Extension." Read it carefully.

20. What is the second of the two properties of simple apprehension we studied in this chapter?

21. What is the answer to the question "What is the extension of the concept 'man'?"

22. What is the answer to the question "What is the extension of the concept 'animal'?"

23. Distinguish between comprehension and extension.

Read "The Relationship between Comprehension and Extension." Read it carefully.

24. Which concept has greater comprehension, 'man' or 'animal'?

25. Which concept has greater extension, 'man' or 'animal'?

26. Which concept has greater extension, 'man' or 'body'?

27. Which concept has greater comprehension, 'man' or 'body'?

28. The greater the comprehension a concept has, the _____________ extension it has; and the more extension it has, the _____________ the comprehension.

_________ Exercises for Day 4.

29. Indicate whether the following statements are true or false:

T	F	The two properties of simple apprehension are concept and extension.
T	F	The concept 'man' is complex.
T	F	Porphyry once said that a man is a "featherless biped."
T	F	If something is sentient, that means that it is something rather than nothing.
T	F	The concept 'man' has four notes.
T	F	The concept 'animal' has greater extension than the concept 'man.'
T	F	The concept 'man' has greater extension than the concept 'body.'
T	F	The concept 'man' has greater comprehension than the concept 'body.'
T	F	The concept 'man' has greater comprehension than the concept 'animal.'

30. Give the comprehension of the concept 'automobile.'

31. Give the extension of the concept 'automobile.'

32. Choose something from your surroundings at home and tell both its comprehension and its extension.

___________ Review Exercises.

33. Indicate whether the following statements are true or false:

T	F	Sense perception is the act of seeing or hearing or smelling or tasting or touching.
T	F	Simple apprehension is an act by which the mind grasps the concept or general meaning of an object and affirms or denies something about it.
T	F	The terms 'concept' and 'simple apprehension' mean the same thing.
T	F	When we have a simple apprehension of a thing, we grasp the thing's essence.
T	F	If we affirm or deny something about a concept, we are going beyond simple apprehension to judgment.

34. Fill out the chart below, listing the mental acts and their corresponding verbal expressions in the order in which we have covered them:

Mental Act	Verbal Expression
■ ____________________	■ ____________________
■ ____________________	■ ____________________
■ ____________________	■ ____________________

Signification and Supposition

Introduction. In the last chapter we discussed the two properties of concepts: comprehension and extension. We said that the ***comprehension*** of a concept was the complete sum of the notes represented by that concept. The comprehension of the concept 'man' is how many notes it has. And we said that the ***extension*** of a concept was the sum of real things to which the concept refers. The extension of the concept 'man' is all the men who are, were, and ever will be.

Comprehension and extension are the two properties of ***concepts***. In this chapter, we will discuss the two properties of ***terms***. Remember that a concept is the *mental act* involved in simple apprehension and a term is the *verbal expression* of that concept. (If need be, go back and review the discussion of this in the Introduction.)

S*ignification* and *supposition* are the two properties of the term.

A term is a word or group of words which verbally expresses a concept.

In the same way that comprehension and extension are the two properties of concepts, ***signification*** and ***supposition*** are the two properties of the term.

Let's talk first about what signification is. We will then discuss supposition. Finally, we will summarize the first three chapters of this book.

Signification. Terms can be divided according to their signification in three ways: there are ***univocal*** terms, ***equivocal*** terms, and ***analogous*** terms.

Univocal terms are terms that have exactly the same meaning no matter when or how they are used. Examples of univocal terms are words and phrases like 'photosynthesis,' 'anthropology,' and 'the second law of thermodynamics.' Other univocal terms would be words and phrases like 'tablesaw,' 'phillips head screwdriver,' and 'drill bit.' Notice that many of these terms are scientific terms or have something to do with manufacturing.

These terms always mean the same thing. They never mean one thing when used by one person on one occasion and another thing when used by somebody else on another occasion.

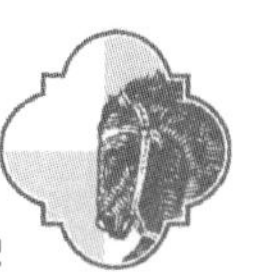

In fact, the word 'univocal' is formed out of two Latin word: 'unus,' which means 'one,' and 'vox,' which means 'voice.' So the term 'univocal' literally means 'one voice.'

Equivocal terms, on the other hand, are terms that, although spelled and pronounced exactly alike, have entirely different and unrelated meanings. Examples of equivocal terms would be words like 'pitcher,' 'plane,' and 'jar.' A pitcher, for example, can be a position in baseball or the thing out of which you pour your orange juice. A plane can be either a figure in geometry or the thing you fly on when you go to Europe. A jar can be a container or a hard knock against something. They are spelled or pronounced the same, but have completely different meanings.

Terms can be divided according to their signification in three ways: there are *univocal* terms, *equivocal* terms, and *analogous* terms.

Equivocal terms are the kinds of words used in puns, which is the humorous use of words that sound alike. When Benjamin Franklin said, "We must all hang together, or assuredly we will all hang separately," he was using the word 'hang' in an equivocal way—it was spelled and pronounced the same, but had completely different meanings. This Franklin quote is a good example of a pun.

The term 'equivocal' also has a Latin origin. It is made up of the word 'aequus,' which means 'equal' and the word 'vox,' which, as we said above, means 'voice.' It means, literally, 'equal voice.' This is a reference to the fact that equivocal terms are pronounced, and many times spelled, the same even though they have different meanings.

Analogous terms are terms that are applied to different things but have related meanings. They are like equivocal terms since they are spelled or pronounced the same but have different meanings. However, unlike equivocal terms, the different meanings they have are related. Examples of analogous terms are words like 'window,' 'wheel,' and 'wooden.' We can speak of a 'window of opportunity,' which is a chance to do something that will not be around for long, or a window in a house. We can speak of a 'set of wheels,' by which I simply mean my car, or a 'set of wheels,' meaning four new tires I intend to put on my car. Likewise, something can be said to be 'wooden,' meaning it is made of wood, or some people can be said to be 'wooden,' meaning that they are not very animated when they speak.

Analogous words fill our language. We use them all the time. They are also heavily used in poetry and literature. For example, when Jesus said, "Follow me; and let the dead bury their dead," he was using the word 'dead' in an analogous way. The first use of it means people who are spiritually dead; the second use of it means people who are physically dead. This is an example of using a word analogously—in two different contexts, but with a related meaning.

How does all this relate to logic? It relates to logic because logic requires an accurate and consistent use of terms. If all terms were univocal—if they mean the same thing no matter when or how they were used—we would never have a problem. But since the English language contains many terms which are equivocal and analogous, we can run into problems if we are not careful.

For example, what if I were to make the following argument:

All NBA basketball players are men
Dennis Rodman is a good NBA basketball player
Therefore, Dennis Rodman is a good man

Now if you follow professional basketball, you know that it is true to say that all NBA basketball players are men. And you also know that it is true to say that Dennis Rodman is a good NBA basketball player. But you also know that Dennis Rodman has intentionally cultivated a sort of "bad boy" image both on and off the court, making it very hard to say that he is a good man. Yet the argument sounds like it is valid—and indeed it is if the term 'good' means the same thing both times it is used.

But, in fact, although the term 'good' looks the same in the second premise and in the conclusion, it is actually used in an analogous way. It has two different (but related) meanings. In the statement:

Dennis Rodman is a good NBA basketball player

the term 'good' means 'athletically proficient,' which Dennis Rodman undoubtedly is, while in the statement:

Therefore, Dennis Rodman is a good man

the term 'good' means 'morally upstanding,' about which (in Rodman's case) there is some doubt.

This is just one example of how the analogous use of a term in an argument can get us into logic trouble. Equivocal terms can also cause logical headaches.

You don't have to fully understand the problem with the argument about Dennis Rodman for now. You will be able to better understand it later. For now, just remember that how we use terms—univocally, equivocally, and analogously—is important in using logic properly.

We should also point out that individual words are not inherently univocal, or equivocal or analogical. The same word may in one circumstance be used one way, and in another circumstance in another way. The same word, in short, may be used univocally in one place, equivocally in another, and analogically in another.

Terms can be divided up according to their *supposition* in three ways: *verbal* existence, *mental* existence and *real* existence.

__________ **Supposition.** Just as there are three ways to divide up terms according to their signification (univocal, equivocal, and analogous), we can also divide terms up according to their ***supposition***.

There are three kinds of existence to which a term can refer. It can refer to ***verbal*** existence, ***mental*** existence, or ***real*** existence. When a term refers to verbal existence, we say it is an instance of ***material*** supposition. When a term refers to mental existence, we say it is an instance of ***logical*** supposition. And when a term refers to real existence, we say it is an instance of ***real*** supposition.

Material supposition occurs when a term refers to something as it exists *verbally*. For example, if we say:

'Man' is a three-letter word

we are using the term 'man' to refer to the word 'man,' rather than the mental idea of a man or any real man. We are using it *verbally*.

Logical supposition occurs when a term refers to something as it exists logically. When we say, for example:

'Man' has five notes

we are using the term 'man' to refer to the mental idea (or concept) of man, rather than to the actual word 'man' (as in material supposition above) or to any real men. We are using it *mentally* or *logically*.

Real supposition occurs when a term refers to something as it exists in the real world. When we say:

Man was created by God

we are using the term 'man' to refer to real men who actually exist in the world, rather than the mental idea of man or to the word 'man.' We are using it *really*.

This chapter is the last chapter that will deal exclusively with terms.

______ **Summary of Chapters 1-3.** This chapter is the last chapter that will deal exclusively with terms. Term, remember, is the first of the three aspects of logic. The three aspects of logic are simple apprehension, judgment, and deductive inference. Remember also that these three aspects of logic are verbally expressed by terms, propositions, and syllogisms. In fact, let's look again at the chart we concluded with in the introduction of this book:

Mental Act	Verbal Expression
Simple Apprehension	Term
Judgment	Proposition
Deductive Inference	Syllogism

In Chapter 1 we dealt with the definition of simple apprehension. In Chapter 2 we dealt with the properties of simple apprehension. In Chapter 3 we dealt with the properties of term. In other words, we stayed on the first step of our chart above.

We said that a term is a word or group of words which stand for a concept which is applicable to real things. The term 'man,' for example, is a word (which has three letters) which stands for a concept (which by comprehension has five notes and by extension refers to all the men who are, ever were, and ever will be) which refers to real men in the world.

In the chapters that follow, we will leave the subject of terms and begin to discuss how terms relate to one another in propositions (or statements).

Once we have completed a study of propositions, we will begin a study of syllogisms (or arguments).

_____________ **Exercises for Day 1.** **Peruse the entire chapter. Then read the introductory section at the very beginning of Chapter 3. Read this section carefully and try to understand it as best you can.**

1. In this chapter, we discussed the two properties of _____________.

2. What is the definition of 'term'?

3. What are the two properties of terms?

Read "Signification." Read the first paragraph carefully.

4. What are the three ways that terms can be divided according to their signification?

_____________ **Exercises for Day 2.** **Read "Signification." Read the entire section carefully.**

5. What are univocal terms?

6. What are some examples of univocal terms mentioned in the section you read for today?

7. Many univocal terms are what kind of terms?

8. What does the term 'univocal' mean if you translate it literally from the Latin?

9. Think up three univocal terms that are not in the book and then write below.

10. What are equivocal terms?

11. What are some examples of equivocal terms mentioned in the section you read for today?

12. In what are many equivocal terms used?

13. What does the term 'equivocal' mean if you translate it literally from the Latin?

14. Think up three equivocal terms that are not in the book and then write below.

15. What are analogous terms?

16. What are some examples of analogous terms mentioned in the section you read for today?

17. In what are analogous terms commonly used?

18. Think up three analogous terms that are not in the book and then write below.

19. Why is it important to know about univocal, equivocal, and analogous terms?

_________ Exercises for Day 3. **Read "Supposition." Read the entire section carefully.**

20. What are the three ways we can divide up terms according to their supposition?

21. What is material supposition?

22. Give an example of material supposition mentioned in the section you read for today.

23. Think up and then write a sentence expressing material supposition not in the book.

24. What is logical supposition?

25. Give an example of logical supposition mentioned in the section you read for today.

26. Think up and then write a sentence expressing logical supposition not in the book.

27. What is real supposition?

28. Give an example of real supposition mentioned in the section you read for today.

29. Think up and then write a sentence expressing real supposition not in the book.

_________ Exercises for Day 4. **Read "Summary of Chapters 1-3." Read it carefully.**

30. Fill out the chart below showing the three aspects of logic:

Mental Act	Verbal Expression
■ ____________	■ ____________
■ ____________	■ ____________
■ ____________	■ ____________

31. With what did Chapter 1 deal?

32. With what did Chapter 2 deal?

33. With what did Chapter 3 deal?

34. Draw lines between the term and the corresponding definition:

Equivocal terms	*terms that have exactly the same meaning no matter when or how they are used*
Univocal terms	*terms that, although spelled and pronounced exactly alike, have entirely different and unrelated meanings*
Analogous terms	*terms that are applied to different things, but have related meanings*

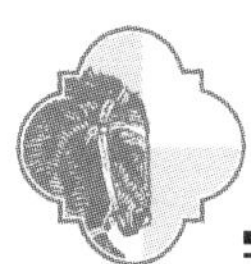

35. Draw lines between the term and the corresponding definition:

Real supposition	*occurs when a term refers to something as it exists verbally*
Logical supposition	*occurs when a term refers to something as it exists logically*
Material supposition	*occurs when a term refers to something as it exists in the real world*

36. Indicate whether the following statements are true or false:

T	F	Comprehension and extension are two properties of terms.
T	F	The three ways terms can be divided according to their signification are univocal, equivocal, and analogous.
T	F	The term 'photosynthesis' is an example of an equivocal term.
T	F	Univocal terms always mean the same thing.
T	F	Equivocal terms have related meanings.
T	F	Analogous terms have entirely different and unrelated meanings.
T	F	The term 'jar' is an example of an equivocal term.
T	F	The term 'window' is an example of an equivocal term.
T	F	Equivocal terms are used in puns.
T	F	Many analogous terms are scientific terms.
T	F	The three ways to divide up terms according to their signification is into verbal, mental, and real existence.
T	F	Material supposition occurs when a term refers to something that exists in the real world.
T	F	When a term refers to real existence, it is said to be an instance of material supposition.
T	F	When a term refers to mental existence, it is said to be an instance of logical supposition.
T	F	In the sentence "Man was created by God," the term 'man' is an example of real supposition.
T	F	The three aspects of logic are simple apprehension, judgment, and deductive inference.

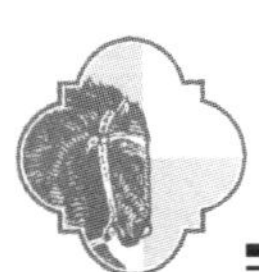

What is Judgment?

Introduction. Now we come to judgment. In the last three chapters we have been discussing ***simple apprehension***, which is a mental act, and ***term***, which is the verbal expression of simple apprehension. Now we turn our attention to the second part of the study of logic.

Just as simple apprehension, as a mental act, has a corresponding verbal expression, so also does judgment. ***Judgment*** is a mental act whose verbal expression is what we call a ***proposition***.

Judgment is the mental act whose verbal expression is what we call a *proposition*.

Let us review the chart we studied in the introductory chapter:

Mental Act	Verbal Expression
Simple Apprehension	Term
Judgment	**Proposition**
Deductive Inference	Syllogism

We see, in this chart, each mental act and its corresponding verbal expression. For judgment, as we have said, the corresponding verbal expression is proposition.

The Definition of Judgment. ***Judgment*** can be defined as ***the act by which the intellect unites by affirming, or separates by denying***. What is it that a judgment unites or separates? A judgment (in categorical propositions) unites or separates two concepts.

When we say, for example, "Man is an animal," we are joining two concepts: the concept 'man' and the concept 'animal.' When we say "Man is *not* God," we are separating the concept 'man' from the concept 'God.'

The two concepts that a judgment unites or separates are called the ***subject*** and the ***predicate***. The subject is that about which we are saying something; it is the concept about which we are affirming or denying something. The predicate is what we are saying about the subject; it is what we are affirming or denying about it.

The statement "Man is an animal," for example, expresses a judgment. In this judgment, the subject is 'man.' It is the concept about which we are going to affirm or deny something. What are we going to affirm or deny about it? In this case, we are affirming that it is an animal. The concept 'animal' is the predicate.

A *proposition* is a sentence or statement which expresses truth or falsity.

———— **The Definition of Proposition.** At its most simple level, as we indicated before, a ***proposition*** can be defined as the verbal expression of a judgment. A more proper definition of proposition, however, would be ***a sentence or statement which expresses truth or falsity.***

Notice that not all sentences are propositions. Only some sentences are propositions. There are, in fact, many sentences that we use in our everyday language which are not propositions and cannot, therefore, be said to express truth or falsity. Questions, commands, exclamations, and greetings are examples of sentences that are not propositions.

When I say, "What is the weather supposed to be like today?" I am not making any claim that you could say was true or false. If I say, "Go to your room" to my son, I am not making any truth claims. The same goes for sentences like "What a nice day!" or "Hello."

But sentences like "It is raining today" or "There is a fly in my soup" do express truth or falsity. They are propositions.

There are three elements of a proposition: the *subject-term*, the *predicate-term*, and the *copula*.

———— **Elements of the Proposition.** There are three elements of any proposition:

the ***subject-term***
the ***predicate-term***
the ***copula***

In our study, we will refer to these as S (the subject-term), P (the predicate-term), and c (the copula). The subject-term is the verbal expression of the subject of a judgment, the predicate-term is the verbal expression of the predicate of a judgment, and the copula is the word in the proposition that connects or relates the subject to the predicate. The copula is some form of the verb 'to be.' The copula is usually expressed by 'is' or 'are.'

In the examples of propositions above, the subject-term is one word and the predicate-term is one word (two, if you count the indefinite article).

Man^{S} is^{c} an animal^{P}

But this is not always the case—far from it. In fact, a subject can contain many words and so can the predicate. For example, we can say:

The little brown-haired boy is very loud.

In this sentence, the subject-term is not just 'boy,' but 'the little brown-haired boy'; and the predicate-term is not just 'loud,' but 'very loud.' The subject-term includes not only 'boy' but all the words that modify 'boy.' The same is true for the predicate.

In other words, the subject-term (S) includes everything we are talking about, and the predicate-term includes everything we are saying about the subject.

___________ **The Logical Form of a Sentence.** Although later on we will discuss the specifics of how to convert a regular proposition that we might use in our everyday language into a more formal logic sentence, let us simply say for now that any sentence we use in logic has to have a certain form. The form it must have in order to be handled logically is called a proposition's ***logical form***.

Let's use a slightly different version of the proposition to which we just made reference to explain what we mean.

The little brown-haired boy screams very loudly.

If we look at this sentence very carefully, let's ask ourselves, "Does this sentence have a subject-term (S), a predicate-term (P), and a copula (c) that are easily distinguished?" In other words, is it easy to tell what S is, what P is, and what c is?

We can easily see that 'the little brown-haired boy' is S (the subject-term). But what about 'screams very loudly'? Which part of this is P (the predicate-term) and which is c (the copula)? It is hard to tell. So what do we do?

What we need to do is to change the wording of this sentence into a form in which S, P, and c are easy to distinguish. In most propositions that are not yet in logical form, the subject is easily distinguished. It is the predicate and the copula that are in need of reworking.

The form which a sentence must be in, in order to be handled logically, is called its *logical form*.

The best way to change such sentences into logical form is to rework the predicate-copula portion of the proposition so that it has a form of the to be verb and a relative clause. For example, we can take the proposition:

The little-brown-haired boy screams very loudly.

and change it to:

The little brown-haired boy *is a child who* screams very loudly.

Notice that this form of the proposition means exactly the same thing as the original version, but it is much easier to tell S, P, and c apart. S is 'the little brown-haired boy'; P is 'a child who screams very loudly,' and c is 'is.'

We will cover more extensively the rules for converting ordinary sentences into clearer logical sentences in a later chapter.

__________ **Summary.** In this chapter, we move from the study of ***simple apprehension*** to the study of ***judgment***. We said that judgment is a mental act whose verbal expression is what we call a ***proposition***. We said that judgment can be defined as the act by which the intellect unites by affirming, or separates by denying. A proposition is a sentence or statement which expresses truth or falsity. The three elements of any proposition are the ***subject-term***, the ***predicate-term***, and the ***copula***. Finally, sentences are much more easily handled in logic if they are put into proper ***logical form***, which means that they must show all three elements of a logical proposition clearly.

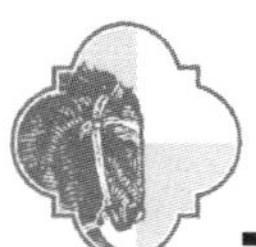

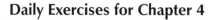

_________ **Exercises for Day 1.** **Peruse the entire chapter. Read the introductory section at the very beginning of Chapter 4. Read this section carefully and try to understand it as best you can.**

1. In the previous chapter, we discussed simple apprehension. What are we discussing in this chapter?

2. What do we call the verbal expression of a simple apprehension? [Review question]

3. What do we call the verbal expression of a judgment?

4. Judgment is the ______________ part of the study of logic.

- first
- second
- third

Read "The Definition of Judgment." Read it carefully.

5. What is the definition of 'judgment'?

6. What does a judgment unite (or separate)?

7. In the sentence "Man is an animal," what two things are we uniting by affirming?

8. In the sentence "Man is not God," what two things are we separating by denying?

9. In any proposition, what are the two concepts which we unite by affirming or separate by denying?

10. Explain what a subject is as we use it in judgment.

11. Explain what a predicate is as we use it in judgment.

12. What is the subject and the predicate in the judgment expressed by the proposition "Man is an animal"?

13. What is the subject and predicate in the judgment expressed by the proposition "Man is not God"?

14. What are we affirming about the subject in the proposition "Man is an animal"?

15. What are we denying about the subject in the proposition "Man is not God"?

_________ **Exercises for Day 2.** **Read "The Definition of Proposition" again. Read the entire section carefully.**

16. What is the proper definition of 'proposition'?

17. What kind of sentences are not propositions?

18. Tell whether the following sentences are propositions or not:

	Proposition	Not a Proposition
Peter is a man.	❐	❐
Just do it.	❐	❐
Where in the world is Carmen San Diego?	❐	❐
Peter is not a man.	❐	❐
There were three thousand purple ducks found on Mars.	❐	❐
Barney (the purple dinosaur) is a man.	❐	❐
Oh, wow!	❐	❐
Hello!	❐	❐
All dogs go to heaven.	❐	❐
No purple dinosaurs go to heaven.	❐	❐
Who is President of the United States?	❐	❐
Barney is President of the United States.	❐	❐
The postman never rings twice.	❐	❐
How are you today?	❐	❐
That's a fine duck you have there.	❐	❐
How many ducks do you have?	❐	❐
Don't feed the animals.	❐	❐
Peter is not a duck.	❐	❐

19. Give three examples of sentences that are propositions.

20. Give six examples of sentences that are *not* propositions.

____________ Exercises for Day 3. **Read "Elements of Propositions." Read the entire section carefully.**

21. What are the three elements of any proposition?

22. Tell what each of the following letters stand for:

S: ____________________________
P: ____________________________
c: ____________________________

23. Explain what the subject-term is.

24. Explain what the predicate-term is.

25. Explain what the copula is.

26. How many words must the subject-term have?

27. How many words must the predicate-term have?

28. Write the subject-term, predicate-term, and copula for each of the following propositions:

Peter is a man.
Two and two are four.
I am the vine.
You are the branches.
I am the Son of God.
My kingdom is not of this world. (Ignore the word 'not' for purposes of this exercise.)

________ Exercises for Day 4. **Read "The Logical Form of a Sentence." Read it carefully.**

29. How do you determine whether a proposition is in logical form?

30. What is the best way to change a sentence that is not in logical form into one that is in logical form?

31. Indicate which of the following sentences are in logical form:

	Logical Form	Not Logical Form
Peter is a man.	❐	❐
My nose is big.	❐	❐
Peter is big.	❐	❐
I am the way and the truth and the life.	❐	❐
He that seeth me seeth Him that sent me.	❐	❐
Man thinks.	❐	❐
Roses are red.	❐	❐
Three's a crowd.	❐	❐
I like it.	❐	❐
Home is where the heart is.	❐	❐

32. Put into logical form the sentences in Question 31 that you identified as not in logical form.

Read "Summary." Read it carefully.

33. Indicate whether the following statements are true or false:

T	F	A proposition is the verbal expression of a judgment.
T	F	A judgment unites two concepts.
T	F	Judgment is the third part of the study of logic.
T	F	The subject and the copula are united by the predicate.
T	F	The subject of the sentence "Man is an animal" is 'animal.'
T	F	The subject of the sentence "Man is not God" is 'God.'
T	F	Questions are not propositions.
T	F	"Just do it" is a proposition.
T	F	"All dogs go to heaven" is a proposition.
T	F	The three elements of any proposition are the subject, the predicate, and the copula.
T	F	A subject-term must have at least two words.

The Four Statements of Logic

Introduction. In the last chapter, we discussed the definition of ***judgment*** and ***proposition***. We said judgment is the act by which the intellect unites by affirming or separates by denying. We said also that a proposition is the verbal expression of a judgment. In this chapter, we will discuss the classification of propositions.

The Four Statements of Logic. In formal logic, there are four basic categorical propositions. (There are other kinds of non-categorical propositions with which formal logic deals, but we will discuss these later in a second book.) They take the following form:

In formal logic, there are four basic categorical propositions.

A: All S is P
I: Some S is P
E: No S is P
O: Some S is not P

As you can see, each of these propositions is indicated by a letter. A stands for the first vowel in ***affirmo***, the Latin word for 'affirm.' That is because the A proposition, "All S is P," affirms something about S; namely, that all S is P.

I stands for the second vowel in ***affirmo***. And that is because it also affirms something about S—not all S's, but some. It says that some S's are P's.

E stands for the first vowel in the word ***nego***, the Latin word for 'negate,' a form of the word 'negative.' That is because it doesn't say anything affirmative about S. It doesn't say what S is. It is negative. It says something about what S is not; namely, S is not P.

O stands for the second vowel in the word ***nego***. It also says something negative about S—not all S's, but some. It says that some S's are not P's.

We are using letters for the subject-term and the predicate-term in these examples. Each one of these propositions is representative of statements we use in real life. Real life examples of these statements would be the following:

All propositions we will use in our study of formal logic will have one of four kinds of quantifiers: *all*, *some*, *no*, or *some ... not*.

A:	All men are mortal; All cars are fast; all boys are rude; All girls are pretty; etc.
I:	Some men are mortal; Some cars are fast; Some boys are rude; Some girls are pretty; etc.
E:	No men are mortal; No cars are fast; No boys are rude; No girls are pretty; etc.
O:	Some men are not mortal; Some cars are not fast; Some boys are not rude; Some girls are not pretty; etc.

__________ **The Quantifier.** We said in the last chapter that propositions had three basic components: the subject-term, the predicate-term, and the copula. In each of the sentences above, you see a subject-term (S), a predicate-term (P), and a copula (the word 'is' and the phrase 'is not'). But there is another component necessary in a logical proposition.

Notice that there is another word in each of the four propositions above. In addition to the subject-term, the predicate-term, and the copula, there is something called a ***quantifier***. In the first proposition, proposition A, the quantifier is 'All'; in proposition I, the quantifier is 'Some'; in proposition E, the quantifier is 'No'; and in proposition O, the quantifier is 'Some ... not.'

All propositions we will use in our study of formal logic will have one of four kinds of quantifiers:

All
Some
No
Some ... not

These quantifiers tell us important things about the propositions in which they appear. They tell us what both the ***quality*** and ***quantity*** of a proposition is. These are the two characteristics of categorical statements.

The quality of a proposition has to do with whether it is *affirmative* or *negative*.

__________ **Quality.** The ***quality*** of a proposition has to do with whether it is ***affirmative*** or ***negative***. In other words, if I ask you the question "What is the quality of this statement?" what I mean is, "Is it affirmative or negative?" If we ask that question of the A proposition—if we ask, in other words, whether it is affirmative or negative—we would say, of course, that it is affirmative. It affirms, rather than denies, something about the subject.

If I say, for example, "All men are mortal," we are affirming something about all men—namely, that they are mortal. Similarly, if we say, "Some men are mortal," we are affirming something about some men—namely, that they are mortal. In both of these kinds of propositions we are affirming something about the subject-term 'men.'

We cannot say the same about statements such as "No men are mortal" or "Some men are not mortal," since in these sentences we are not affirming anything about the subject 'men'; rather, we are denying something about the subject.

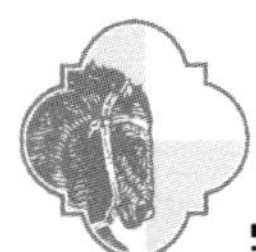

The first two kinds of statements, which are A and I statements, are said to be *affirmative*. The second two kinds of statements, which are E and O statements, are said to be *negative*.

Again, whether a proposition is affirmative or negative is a question of ***quality***.

__________ **Quantity.** But there is another characteristic about these statements that is important for logical purposes. We cannot only ask about the quality of a proposition, but also about its quantity. The ***quantity*** of a proposition has to do with whether it is ***universal*** or ***particular***. A proposition is universal if it says something about *all* of the members of the class referred to by the subject of the proposition. A proposition is particular if it says something about only *some* members of the class referred to by the subject of the sentence.

In other words, if I ask you the question "What is the quantity of this statement?" what I mean is, "Is it universal or particular?" If we ask that question of the A proposition—if we ask, in other words, whether it is universal or particular—we would say, of course, that it is universal. It refers to all A's, not just some.

The quantity of a proposition has to do with whether it is *universal* or *particular*.

If we say, for example, "All men are mortal," we are affirming something about all men—namely, that they are mortal. Similarly, if we say, "No men are mortal," we are denying something about all men—namely, we are denying that they are mortal. In both of these kinds of propositions we are saying something about all the members of the subject-class 'men.' These kinds of statements are said to be ***universal***.

We cannot say the same about statements such as "Some men are mortal" or "Some men are not mortal," since in these statements we are not affirming something about all men, nor are we denying something about all men. We are affirming or denying something about only some men. These kinds of statements are said to be ***particular***.

__________ **Distinguishing Universal Statements.** Many statements have no quantifier. In these cases, we must try to determine, without benefit of a quantifier, whether the statements are universal or particular. For example, if we say, "Frogs are ugly," we likely have in mind the idea that *all* frogs are ugly. Therefore, we could easily rewrite such a statement to say just that: "All frogs are ugly."

The general rule for statements that do not contain a quantifier is that *all* is intended, unless *some* is clearly indicated.

If, for example, we hear someone say, "Men have gone to the North Pole," we can clearly see, even though the word 'some' is not expressed in the statement, that the speaker does not really mean that *all* men have gone to the North Pole. It is pretty clear that what the statement really means is, "Some men have gone to the North Pole."

There are also statements in which the subject-term indicated is an individual. When we say, for example, "Socrates is a man," we see that the subject-term is 'Socrates.' Is it universal or particular? These types of statements are called ***singular*** statements. There are cases in which particular statements are treated differently from universal statements, but we will not encounter any of these in this book, and so we will treat them as universal statements.

We can do this without much difficulty since what we wish to indicate is that every person indicated by the term 'Socrates' is a man. In the statement we are, of course, talking about only one individual. Although there may have been more than one individual named Socrates, our statement is about only one of them. The statement is universal in the sense that everyone we mean when we use the subject-term 'Socrates' (which happens to be a single person) is a man. In this sense the statement is universal. This goes for any statement in which the subject-term is the name of a person and a certain individual is obviously meant.

The general rule for statements that do not contain a quantifier is that *all* is intended, unless *some* is clearly indicated.

Summary. Let us summarize what we have learned in this chapter.

We said first that there are four basic categorical propositions with which formal logic deals: "All S is P"; "Some S is P"; "No S is P"; and "Some S is not P." We noted that, in addition to the three components, the subject-term (S), the predicate-term (P), and the copula (is), there is a fourth component: the quantifier. The quantifiers are the words 'All,' 'Some,' 'No,' and 'Some ... not.'

We said that there are two fundamental characteristics of categorical propositions: quality and quantity. ***Quality*** has to do with whether a statement is ***affirmative*** or ***negative***. ***Quantity*** has to do with whether a proposition is ***universal*** or ***particular***.

A and I statements are affirmative, while E and O statements are negative; this is their quality. A and E statements are universal, while I and O statements are particular; this is their quantity.

We can summarize the quality and quantity of each statement as follows:

A: Affirmative-Universal
I: Affirmative-Particular
E: Negative-Universal
O: Negative-Particular

See Figure 5-1 for a diagram of these characteristics of categorical propositions.

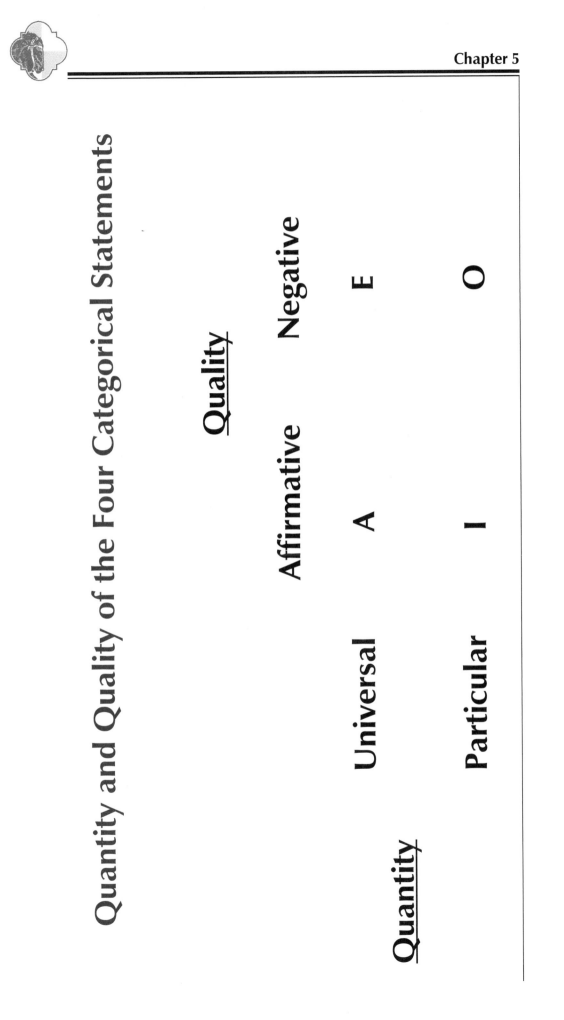

Quantity and Quality of the Four Categorical Statements

		Quality	
		Affirmative	Negative
Quantity	Universal	A	E
	Particular	I	O

Figure 5-1

_________ **Exercises for Day 1. Peruse the entire chapter. Then read the introductory section at the very beginning of Chapter 5. Read this section carefully and try to understand it as best you can.**

1. What are we discussing in this chapter?

Read "The Four Statements of Logic." Read it carefully.

2. What are the four basic categorical propositions? (Use S to represent the subject-term and P to represent the predicate-term in each proposition.)

3. What are the letters that we use to represent each of these propositions?

4. Why is "All S is P" called an A statement?

5. Why is "Some S is P" called an I statement?

6. Why is "No S is P" called an E statement?

7. Why is "Some S is not P" called an O statement?

8. Tell whether the following are A, I, E, or O statements:

_____ All men are mortal.
_____ Some men are not mortal.
_____ No boys are rude.
_____ All cars are fast.
_____ Some men are mortal.
_____ Some boys are rude.
_____ No men are mortal.
_____ Some boys are not rude.

_____ No girls are pretty.
_____ Some cars are not fast.
_____ All boys are rude.
_____ Some girls are not pretty.
_____ All girls are pretty.
_____ Some cars are fast.
_____ No cars are fast.
_____ Some girls are pretty.

Read "The Quantifier." Read it carefully.

9. In addition to the subject-term, the predicate-term, and the copula, what is the fourth component of a categorical proposition?

10. What are the four quantifiers used in categorical statements?

11. Indicate the quantifier in the following statements:

All men are mortal.
Some men are mortal.
No men are mortal.
Some men are not mortal.

12. Indicate the quantifier in each of the statements in Question 8.

13. What are the two characteristics of categorical statements?

________ Exercises for Day 2. Read "Quality." Read it carefully.

14. With what does the quality of a proposition have to do?

15. What are we asking when we ask, "What is the quality of this statement?"?

16. What do we mean when we say that a proposition is affirmative?

17. What do we mean when we say that a proposition is negative?

18. Indicate whether each of the following categorical statements is affirmative or negative:

    All S is P
    Some S is P
    No S is P
    Some S is not P

19. Indicate whether each of the following categorical statements is affirmative or negative:

    All men are mortal.
    Some men are not mortal.
    No boys are rude.
    All cars are fast.
    Some men are mortal.
    Some boys are rude.
    No men are mortal.
    Some boys are not rude.
    No girls are pretty.
    Some cars are fast.
    All boys are rude.
    Some girls are not pretty.
    All girls are pretty.
    Some cars are fast.
    No cars are fast.
    Some girls are pretty.

20. Think up five affirmative propositions that are not in the book.

21. Think up five negative propositions that are not in the book.

________ Exercises for Day 3. Read "Quantity." Read the entire section carefully.

22. With what does the quantity of a proposition have to do?

23. What are we asking when we ask, "What is the quantity of this statement?"?

24. What do we mean when we say that a proposition is universal?

25. What do we mean when we say that a proposition is particular?

26. Indicate whether each of the following categorical statements is universal or particular:

    All S is P
    Some S is P
    No S is P
    Some S is not P

27. Indicate whether each of the following categorical statements is universal or particular:

All men are mortal.
Some men are not mortal.
No boys are rude.
All cars are fast.
Some men are mortal.
Some boys are rude.
No men are mortal.
Some boys are not rude.

No girls are pretty.
Some cars are fast.
All boys are rude.
Some girls are not pretty.
All girls are pretty.
Some cars are fast.
No cars are fast.
Some girls are pretty.

28. Think up five universal sentences that are not in the book.

29. Think up five particular sentences that are not in the book.

__________ Exercises for Day 4. **Read "Distinguishing Universal Statements." Read the entire section carefully.**

30. What is the rule for distinguishing universal statements?

31. Are statements in which the subject-term is the name of a certain individual universal or particular? Explain.

32. Tell which of the following statements are universal and which are particular:

Caesar is a great general.
Mary is the mother of Jesus.
The soldiers are tired.
Jesus is the Son of God.
Christians pray.
Albert Einstein was a genius.
Romans are cruel.

Read "Summary." Read the entire section carefully.

33. Tell the quality and quantity of each proposition:

All kings are good.
No truth is simple.
Some generals are great.
Some Gauls are not brave.
All Romans are brave.
Some wars are not cruel.
All Christians are brothers.
No wars are peaceful.

Some towns are well-fortified.
All truth is God's truth.
Some towns are not fortified.
Some victories are not glorious.
No tribes are safe.
All leaders are slaughtered.
Some wars are fierce.
No kings are good.

34. Fill out the following chart: ___________

		Affirmative	Negative
	Universal	_____	_____
_________			
	Particular	_____	_____

_________ Review Exercises for Day 4.

35. What is the best way to change a sentence that is not in logical form into one that is in logical form?

36. Indicate whether the following statements are true or false:

T	F	A proposition is the verbal expression of a judgment.
T	F	Judgment is the third part of the study of logic.
T	F	The subject and the copula are united by the predicate.
T	F	"Just do it" is a proposition.
T	F	"All dogs go to heaven" is a proposition.
T	F	A subject-term must have at least two words.

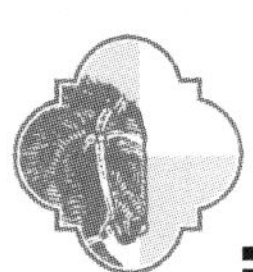

Contradictory and Contrary Statements

Introduction. In the last chapter, we dealt with the four kinds of categorical statements: A, I, E, and O statements. In this chapter, we will deal with the first kind of relationship that these statements can have to one another.

There are two relationships categorical statements can have to one another. The first is the relationship of ***opposition***. The second is the relationship of ***equivalence***. There are four different kinds of opposing relationships and three different kinds of equivalent relationships. In this chapter, we will discuss the first two of the four different relationships of opposition.

When we use the term 'opposition,' we mean the relationship which we observe in things we call 'opposite.' If we say something is the opposite of another thing, we are saying the two things have a relationship of opposition. Statements that are in opposition *affirm* and *deny* the same predicate of the same subject.

Statements that are in opposition *affirm* and *deny* the same predicate of the same subject.

There are four ways that any two of these four statements—A, I, E, and O—can be related in opposition. In other words, any one of these statements can be said to be opposite to another in any one of four different ways. They can be ***contradictory*** to one another; they can be ***contrary*** to one another; they can be ***subcontrary***; and they can be ***subalternate***. We will discuss only contradictory and contrary statements in this chapter and leave subcontrary and subalternate statements until the next chapter.

The Rule of Contradiction. Let us begin the discussion of contradiction by articulating the ***Rule of Contradiction***:

> ***Contradictory statements are statements that differ in both quality and quantity.***

What does this mean?

If you remember, we set up a chart in Figure 5-1 to illustrate the four statements in terms of their quality and quantity. Using Figure 5-1 as the foundation, let us recreate this chart as Figure 6-1.

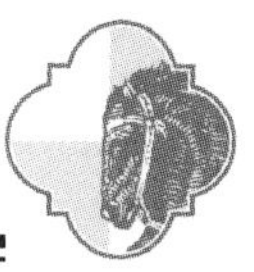

As you can see, if you look at this chart, we have shown each of the four statements in a way that shows us both its quality and quantity. If we were to take our Rule of Contradiction and apply it, we would look at this chart and ask ourselves, "Which are the statements that differ in quality and quantity?"

Let us consider first the A statement, "All S is P." What is the quality of the A statement? In other words, is it affirmative or negative? If you look at your chart, you will see that the quality of A is affirmative. It affirms something about S—namely, that it is P.

What is the quantity of the A statement? In other words, is it universal or particular? Does it affirm something about all A's or just some of them? In Figure 6-1, you can see that the quantity of A is universal. It says something about all S's—namely, that they are P's.

Therefore, the quality of the A statement is affirmative. The quantity is universal. Which of the other three propositions, the I, E, or O statements, are contradictory to A? We know that whichever statement it is has to differ from A in quality and quantity. In other words, it has to be negative (since A is affirmative) and particular (since A is universal). Which of the other three propositions is negative and particular? If we look again at Figure 6-1, we see that it is the O proposition, "Some S is not P." The O proposition is negative and particular. Since it differs from A in both quality and quantity, it is said to be contradictory to A.

Contradictory statements are statements that differ in both quality and quantity.

Now let us look at the E statement, "No S is P." What is the quality of the E statement? In other words, is it affirmative or negative? We see that it is negative; since it does not affirm, it denies. What is the quantity of the E statement? In other words, is it universal or particular? It is universal, since it denies something of all S's, not just some of them. Therefore, the E statement is negative and universal.

Which of the other statements, A, I, or O, is contradictory to E? In other words, which one of these differs from the E statement in both quality and quantity? Which statement is both affirmative (since E is negative) and particular (since E is universal)? If we look at Figure 6-1, we see that it is the I statement. The I statement is both affirmative and particular, making it differ from the E statement in both quality and quantity. We may conclude, then, that the E and I statements are contradictory to one another.

We have determined, then, that A and O statements are contradictory and E and I statements are contradictory. We can see this graphically illustrated in Figure 6-2.

Notice that while A and O statements and E and I statements are contradictory to one another, they are the only two contradictory pairs of statements. A and I statements are not contradictory to one another, nor are E and O statements, nor I and O statements, nor A and E statements.

Quantity and Quality of the Four Categorical Statements

		Quality	
		Affirmative	Negative
Quantity	Universal	A (All S is P)	E (No S is P)
	Particular	I (Some S is P)	O (Some S is not *P*)

Figure 6-1

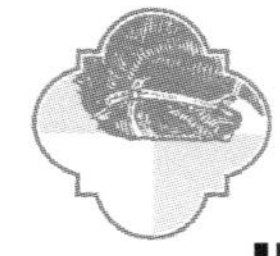

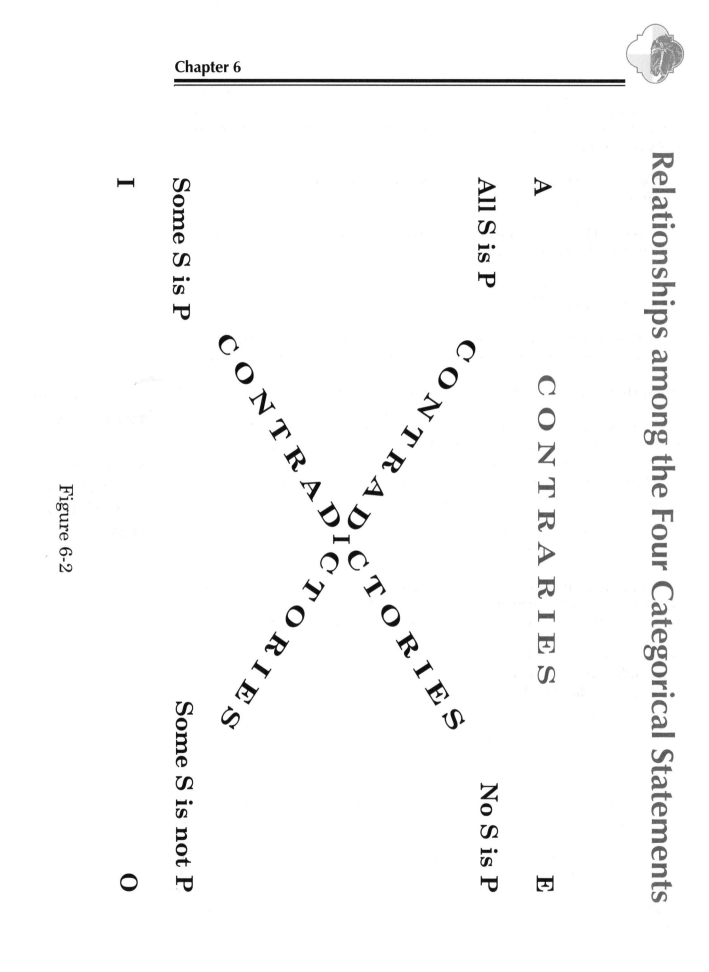

Relationships among the Four Categorical Statements

Figure 6-2

_____________ **The First Law of Opposition.** Let us now explore a little more what contradiction means. Let's start by first setting down the ***First Law of Opposition***:

> ***Contradictories cannot at the same time be true nor at the same time be false.***

In order to further explain this rule, let us look at one pair of contradictories. Let's use the A and O statements:

A: All S is P
O: Some S is not P

Is there any way both can be true or both false at the same time? If it is true to say that all S is P, can it also be true to say that some S is not P? No. If all S is P, like statement A indicates, then there can be no S that is not P. But the O statement says that there is some S that is not P. So they can't both be true.

Furthermore, if it is false to say that all S is P, can it also be false to say that some S is not P? No. If not all S is P, then some S must not be P, just like the O statement says. In other words, if the A statement is false, then the O statement must be true. They cannot both be false at the same time.

Let's try it on some other statements:

A: All men are mortal
O: Some men are not mortal

Can both of these statements be true? If all men are mortal, as in statement A, then there can be no men who are not mortal. But the O statement says that some men are not mortal. So they cannot both be true. And if it is false to say that all men are mortal, then there must be some men who are not mortal, which is just what statement O says. So they can't both be false. They can't both be true at the same time, and they can't both be false at the same time—just as the First Law of Opposition says.

What about E and I statements?

E: No men are gods
I: Some men are gods

Can they both be true? If no men are gods, as in statement E, then we can't very well say that some men are gods. But the I statement says that some men are gods. Therefore, they cannot both be true. And if it is false to say that some men are gods, then there must not be any men who are gods, which is just what statement E says, "No men are gods." So they cannot both be false at the same time. They cannot both be true at the same time, and they cannot both be false at the same time. Again, the First Law of Opposition has proved true.

Contradictory statements cannot at the same time be true nor at the same time be false.

The A and E statements at first seem like they are contradictory. To say, "All S is P" seems as if it should be contradictory to "No S is P," but it is not. A and E statements are opposed to one another, but not by contradiction.

The Rule of Contraries says that two statements are contrary to one another if they are both universals but differ in quality.

__________ **The Rule of Contraries.** ***The Rule of Contraries*** says the following:

> ***Two statements are contrary to one another if they are both universals but differ in quality.***

Whereas there were two combinations of statements that we found to be contradictory, there is only one combination of statements that is contrary.

We see immediately that the only two statements that are universal are A, "All S is P," and E, "No S is P." And as you can see, although they are both universal, one is affirmative and one is negative. They are the same in quantity, but they differ in quality. They must therefore be contrary. You can see that the relationship between these two statements indicated on Figure 6-2.

__________ **The Second Law of Opposition.** ***The Second Law of Opposition*** applies to contraries. It says:

> ***Contraries cannot at the same time both be true, but can at the same time both be false.***

If "All S is P" is true, then "No S is P" must be false. And if "No S is P" is true, then "All S is P" must be false. But if "All S is P" is false, we don't know whether "No S is P" is true or false, because both could be false at the same time.

If someone told us, for example, "All men are white," and someone else told us, "No men are white," we know it would be impossible for both to be true. But they might both be false. They would both be false, for example, if some men were white and some black. We know that in the real world this is in fact the case. Some men are white and some are black.

__________ **Summary.** Let us summarize what we have learned in this chapter. We learned first that, according to the ***Rule of Contradiction***, two statements are contradictory if they differ in both quality and quantity. Second, according to the ***First Law of Opposition***, two contradictory statements cannot both be true at the same time, nor can they both be false at the same time.

The Rule of Contradiction is the test you apply to determine whether two statements are contradictory. The First Law of Opposition tells us an essential characteristic of the relationship between contradictory statements.

If you ever get confused about which statements are contradictory, all you have to do is remember that they must differ in both quality and quantity—and that they are diagonal to each other on the chart (Figure 6-2). We learned also that, according to the ***Rule of Contraries***, two statements are contrary if they are both universal but differ in quality. Second, according to the ***Second Law of Opposition***, two contraries cannot both be true at the same time, but can at the same time both be false.

Again, if you ever get confused about which statements are contrary, all you have to do is remember that they must both be universal but differ in quality—and that they are indicated on the chart (Figure 6-2).

_________ **Exercises for Day 1. Peruse the entire chapter. Then read the introductory section at the very beginning of Chapter 6. Read this section carefully and try to understand it as best you can.**

1. What are the two kinds of relationships statements can have to one another?

2. What do we mean in logic when we speak of 'opposition'?

3. What are we doing when we oppose propositions?

4. What are the four ways A, I, E, and O statements can be related to one another in opposition?

Read "The Rule of Contradiction." Read it carefully.

5. Express the Rule of Contradiction.

6. Tell the quality and quantity of the A statement.

7. Tell the quality and quantity of the O statement.

8. Does the A statement contradict the O statement? If so, explain why; if not, explain why not.

9. Which other pair of statements is contradictory to one another?

10. Indicate which of the following pairs of statements are contradictory to one another by writing a *C* between each pair of contradictory statements:

All logic problems are difficult.	_____	Some logic problems are difficult.
No logic problems are difficult.	_____	All logic problems are difficult.
Some logic problems are difficult.	_____	No logic problems are difficult.
Some logic problems are not difficult.	_____	All logic problems are difficult.
All logic problems are difficult.	_____	No logic problems are difficult.
No logic problems are difficult.	_____	Some logic problems are not difficult.
Some logic problems are difficult.	_____	Some logic problems are not difficult.
Some men are white.	_____	Some men are not white.
No men are white.	_____	Some men are not white.
All men are white.	_____	No men are white.
Some men are not white.	_____	All men are white.
Some men are white.	_____	No men are white.
No men are white.	_____	All men are white.
All men are white.	_____	Some men are white.

_________ **Exercises for Day 2. Read "The First Law of Opposition." Read it carefully.**

11. What is the First Law of Opposition?

12. Can both A and O statements be true at the same time?

13. Can both A and O statements be false at the same time?

14. Can both E and I statements be true at the same time?

15. Can both E and I statements be false at the same time?

16. Which two pairs of statements are affected by the First Law of Opposition?

17. Indicate which of the following pairs of statements are contradictory by writing a *C* between each pair of contradictory statements:

No cars are fast.	______	All cars are fast.
Some omelettes are tasty.	______	No omelettes are tasty.
Some tomatoes are not red.	______	All tomatoes are red.
Michael Jordan is a good basketball player.	______	Michael Jordan is not a good basketball player.
No guns are loud.	______	Some guns are not loud.
Some rocks are crystals.	______	Some rocks are not crystals.
Some men are sinners.	______	Some men are not sinners.
No men are saved.	______	Some men are not saved.
All wars are bloody.	______	No wars are bloody.
Some soldiers are not brave.	______	All soldiers are brave.
Some animals are amphibians.	______	No animals are amphibians.
No houses are well-built.	______	All houses are well-built.
All storms are violent.	______	Some storms are violent.
All machines are loud.	______	Some machines are loud.

18. Explain why the A statement "All S is P" and the E statement "No S is P" are not contradictory.

__________ Exercises for Day 3. **Read "The Rule of Contraries." Read it carefully.**

19. Express the Rule of Contraries.

20. Tell the quality and quantity of the A statement.

21. Tell the quality and quantity of the E statement.

22. Is the A statement contrary to the E statement? If so, explain why; if not, explain why not.

23. Are there any other pairs of statements that are contrary to one another? If so, indicate which they are.

24. Indicate which of the following pairs of statements are contrary (not contradictory) to one another by writing a *C* between each pair of contrary statements:

All logic problems are difficult.	_____	Some logic problems are difficult.
No logic problems are difficult.	_____	All logic problems are difficult.
Some logic problems are difficult.	_____	No logic problems are difficult.
Some logic problems are not difficult.	_____	All logic problems are difficult.
All logic problems are difficult.	_____	No logic problems are difficult.
No logic problems are difficult.	_____	Some logic problems are not difficult.
Some logic problems are difficult.	_____	Some logic problems are not difficult.
Some men are white.	_____	Some men are not white.
No men are white.	_____	Some men are not white.
All men are white.	_____	No men are white.
Some men are not white.	_____	All men are white.
Some men are white.	_____	No men are white.
No men are white.	_____	All men are white.
All men are white.	_____	Some men are white.

Read "The Second Law of Opposition." Read it carefully.

25. What is the Second Law of Opposition?

26. Which pair of statements comply with the Second Law of Opposition?

27. Indicate which of the following pairs of statements are contrary by writing a *C* between each pair of contrary statements:

No cars are fast.	______	All cars are fast.
Some omelettes are tasty.	______	No omelettes are tasty.
Some tomatoes are not red.	______	All tomatoes are red.
Michael Jordan is a good basketball player.	______	Michael Jordan is not a good basketball player.
No guns are loud.	______	Some guns are not loud.
Some rocks are crystals.	______	Some rocks are not crystals.
Some men are sinners.	______	Some men are not sinners.
No men are saved.	______	Some men are not saved.
All wars are bloody.	______	No wars are bloody.
Some soldiers are not brave.	______	All soldiers are brave.
Some animals are amphibians.	______	No animals are amphibians.
No houses are well-built.	______	All houses are well-built.
All storms are violent.	______	Some storms are violent.
All machines are loud.	______	Some machines are loud.

28. Explain why the A statement "All S is P" and the O statement "Some S is not P" are not contrary.

29. Explain why the I statement "Some S is P" and the E statement "No S is P" are not contrary.

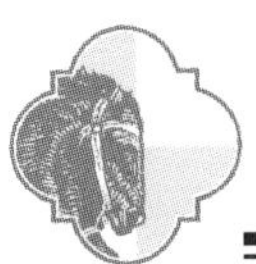

________ Exercises for Day 4. Read "Summary." Read the entire section carefully.

30. Fill out the following chart: ___________

		Affirmative	Negative
	Universal	_____	_____
_________			
	Particular	_____	_____

31. In the following chart, indicate, as in Figure 6-2, which two pairs of statements are contradictory and which two statements are contrary:

A	E
I	O

32. Write five pairs of contradictory statements that are not in the book.

33. Write five pairs of contrary statements that are not in the book.

34. Indicate whether the following statements are true or false:

T	F	Two statements are contradictory if they differ from each other in quality, but are the same in quantity.
T	F	The quality of the statement "All S is P" is universal.
T	F	The quantity of the statement "Some S is P" is particular.
T	F	The A statement and the O statement differ in quality and quantity.
T	F	The statements "All S is P" and "No S is P" can both be true at the same time.
T	F	The statements "All S is P" and "No S is P" can both be false at the same time.
T	F	The A statement and the E statement are not contradictory because, although they differ in quality, they do not differ in quantity.
T	F	The statement "Just do it" and the statement "All men are mortal" are contradictory.
T	F	The statements "All football players are big" and "No football players are big" are contrary.
T	F	Contrary statements cannot at the same time be false, but they can both be true.

________ Review Exercises for Day 4.

35. What do we call the verbal expression of a judgment?

36. How do you determine whether a proposition is in logical form?

37. Are statements in which the subject-term is the name of a certain individual universal or particular? Explain.

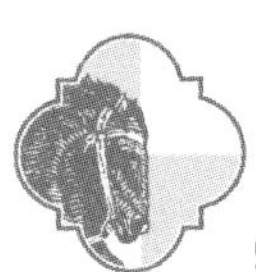

Subcontraries and Subalterns

Introduction. Remember that in the last chapter we said that there are four ways that any two of the four statements—A, I, E, and O—can be related in opposition. In other words, any one of these statements can be said to be opposite to another of them in any one of four different ways. They can be ***contradictory*** to one another, they can be ***contrary*** to one another, they can be ***subcontrary***, and they can be ***subalternate***.

In the last chapter we studied the first two of the four kinds of opposition between categorical statements. We studied contradiction and contrariness. In this chapter, we will discuss subcontrariness and subalternation, the last two of the four kinds of opposition.

Two statements are subcontrary if they are both particular statements that differ in quality.

The Rule of Subcontraries. Let us begin by articulating the ***Rule of Subcontraries***:

> ***Two statements are subcontrary if they are both particular statements that differ in quality.***

The difference between contraries and subcontraries is that, while two contrary statements are both universal, two statements that are subcontrary are both particular. Two statements that are subcontrary are both particular, but one is affirmative and one is negative.

Of the four statements we have been discussing—A, I, E, and O—which one is particular and affirmative? "Some S is P," the I statement, is particular and affirmative. Of the four statements, which one is particular and negative? "Some S is not P," the O statement, is particular and negative. Therefore, the I and the O statements are subcontrary.

Let's take a look again at our chart showing the ***Square of Opposition***. Look at Figure 7-1. If we look at the chart and ask ourselves, "Which statements are particular but differ in quality?" we see that they are the two bottom statements, I and O.

Like contraries, but unlike contradictories, there is only one combination of statements that are subcontrary. The two contrary statements are A and E. The two subcontrary statements are I and O.

Relationships among the Four Categorical Statements

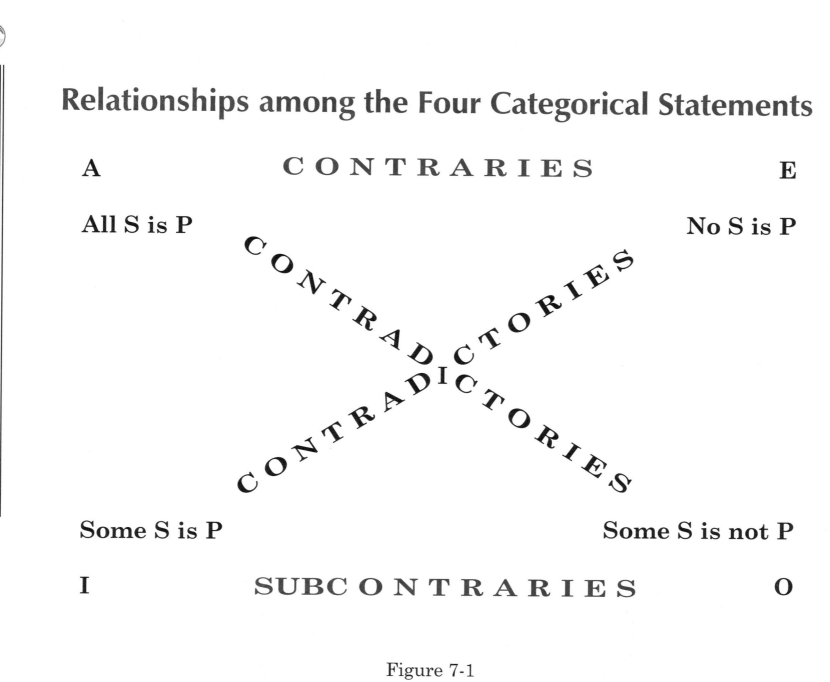

Figure 7-1

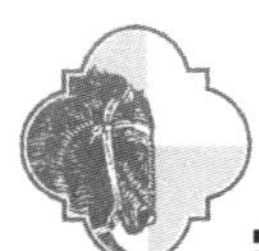

__________ **The Third Law of Opposition.** Let us now explore a little more what subcontrariness means. Let's start by defining the ***Third Law of Opposition:***

> ***Subcontraries may at the same time both be true, but cannot at the same time both be false.***

If one is false, the other must be true. If one is true, then the other may be either true or false. Look at the following statements:

I: Some S is P
O: Some S is not P

Subcontraries may at the same time both be *true*, but cannot at the same time both be *false*.

If one is false, is there any way the other can be false as well? If one is true, does that require that the other be either true or false? If I say "Some men are mortal" and that statement is false, then it would be impossible for the statement "Some men are not mortal" to be false too. If "Some men are mortal" is false, then we know that no men are mortal. And if no men are mortal, then "Some men are not mortal" cannot be false.

__________ **The Rule of Subalterns.** ***The Rule of Subalterns*** says the following:

> ***Two statements are subalternate if they have the same quality, but differ in quantity.***

They are propositions with the same subject, predicate, and copula, one of which is universal and the other particular.

Unlike contradictories, contraries, and subcontraries, subalterns are really not opposite to one another. But they do have a particular logical relationship with one another that helps to complete the Square of Opposition.

Whereas there was only one combination of statements that we found to be contrary and subcontrary, there are (like contradictories) two combinations of statements that are subalternate.

Two statements are subalternate if they have the same quality, but differ in quantity.

We see in Figure 7-2 that there are two pairs of statements that have the same quality but differ in quantity. First, the A statement and the I statement have the same quality (they are both affirmative), but they differ in quantity (one, A, is universal, while the other, I, is particular). A and I, therefore, are subalterns.

Second, we notice that the E statement and the O statement have the same quality (they are both negative), but they differ in quantity (one, E, is universal, while the other, O, is particular). E and O, therefore, are subalterns.

__________ **The Fourth Law of Opposition.** ***The Fourth Law of Opposition*** applies to subalterns. It says:

> ***Subalterns may both be true or both be false. If the particular is false, the universal is false; if the universal is true, then the particular is true; otherwise, their status is indeterminate.***

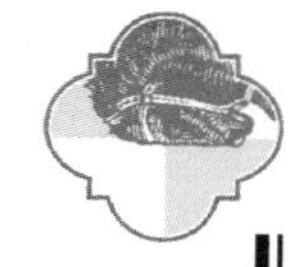

Relationships among the Four Categorical Statements

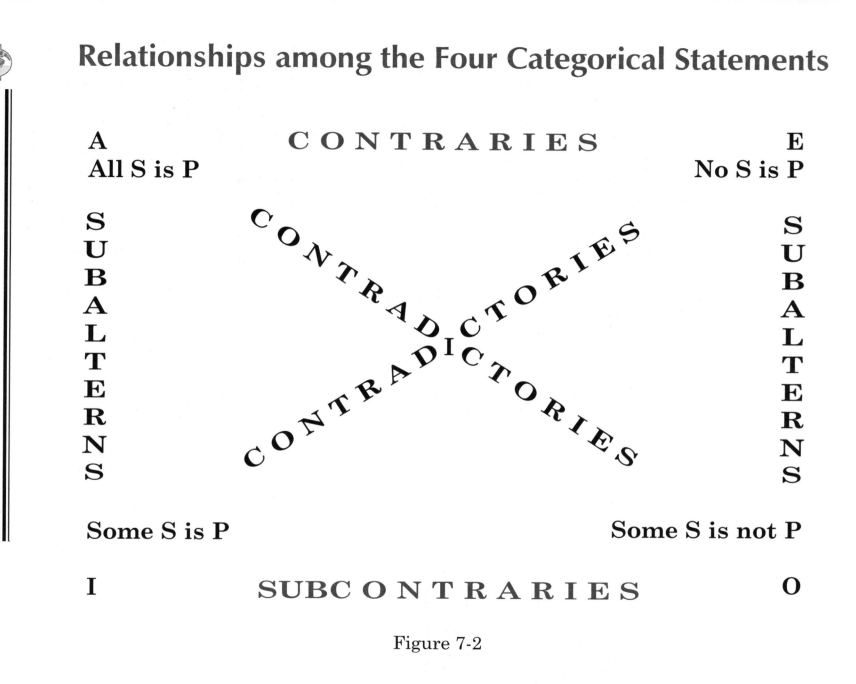

Figure 7-2

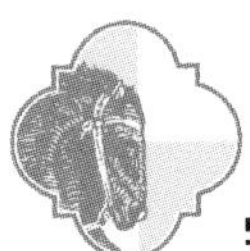

In other words, when it comes to A and I statements, if "Some S is P" is false, then we know that "All S is P" is false. And if "All S is P" is true, then we know that "Some S is P" is true. It also works with E and O statements, since they, too, are subalterns. If "Some S is not P" is false, then "No S is P" must be false. And if "No S is P" is true, then "Some S is not P" must be true.

When we say, in the Fourth Law of Opposition, "otherwise, their status is indeterminate," what we mean is (in the case of A and I statements) if "All S is P" is false, we cannot know whether "Some S is P" is true or false. And if "Some S is P" is true, we cannot know whether "All S is P" is true or false. And (in the case of E and O statements, which are also subalterns) if "No S is P" is false, we cannot know whether "Some S is not P" is true or false, and if "Some S is not P" is true, we cannot know whether "No S is P" is true or false.

If we said, for example, "All men are white," then we know it must be true to say that "Some men are white." But if we know that "Some men are white," we don't necessarily know that "All men are white." Likewise, if we know that "No men are white," then we also know that "Some men are not white" (since some merely means more than one). But if "Some men are not white," we don't necessarily know that "No men are white."

Summary. Let us summarize what we have learned in the last two chapters. We learned in the last chapter that, according to the ***Rule of Contradiction***, two statements are contradictory if they differ in both quality and quantity. According to the ***First Law of Opposition***, two contradictory statements cannot both be true at the same time, nor can they both be false at the same time.

We also learned in the last chapter that, according to the ***Rule of Contraries***, two statements are contrary if they are both universal but differ in quality. According to the ***Second Law of Opposition***, two contraries cannot both be true at the same time, but can, at the same time, both be false.

According to the ***Rule of Subcontraries***, two statements are subcontrary if they are both particular statements that differ in quality. According to the ***Third Law of Opposition***, two subcontraries may at the same time be true, but cannot at the same time be false.

We learned that, according to the ***Rule of Subalterns***, two statements are subalternate if they have the same quality, but differ in quantity. According to the ***Fourth Law of Opposition***, subalterns may both be true or both be false. If the particular is false, the universal is false; if the universal is true, then the particular is true; otherwise their status is indeterminate.

If you ever get confused about which statements are contradictory, contrary, subcontrary, or subalternate, all you have to do is consult Figure 7-2, where all the relationships are visually illustrated.

Subalterns may both be true or both be false. If the particular is false, the universal is false; if the universal is true, then the particular is true; otherwise, their status is indeterminate.

_________ **Exercises for Day 1.** **Peruse the entire chapter. Read the introductory section at the very beginning of Chapter 7. Read this section carefully and try to understand it as best you can.**

1. What are the four ways A, I, E, and O statements can be related to one another in opposition?

2. With which two of these is this chapter concerned?

Read "The Rule of Subcontraries." Read it carefully.

3. Express the Rule of Subcontraries.

4. Tell the quality and quantity of the I statement.

5. Tell the quality and quantity of the O statement.

6. Is the I statement subcontrary to the O statement? If so, explain why; if not, explain why not.

7. Which other pair of statements are subcontrary to one another?

8. Indicate which of the following pairs of statements are subcontrary to one another by writing an *S* between each pair of subcontrary statements:

All logic problems are difficult.	_____	Some logic problems are difficult.
No logic problems are difficult.	_____	All logic problems are difficult.
Some logic problems are difficult.	_____	No logic problems are difficult.
Some logic problems are not difficult.	_____	All logic problems are difficult.
All logic problems are difficult.	_____	No logic problems are difficult.
No logic problems are difficult.	_____	Some logic problems are not difficult.
Some logic problems are difficult.	_____	Some logic problems are not difficult.
Some men are white.	_____	Some men are not white.
No men are white.	_____	Some men are not white.
All men are white.	_____	No men are white.
Some men are not white.	_____	All men are white.
Some men are white.	_____	No men are white.
No men are white.	_____	All men are white.
All men are white.	_____	Some men are white.

_________ **Exercises for Day 2.** **Read "The Third Law of Opposition." Read it carefully.**

9. What is the Third Law of Opposition?

10. Can both I and O statements be true at the same time?

11. Can both I and O statements be false at the same time?

12. Which pair of statements complies with the Third Law of Opposition?

13. Indicate which of the following pairs of statements are subcontrary by writing an *S* between each pair of subcontrary statements:

No cars are fast.	_____	All cars are fast.
Some omelettes are tasty.	_____	No omelettes are tasty.
Some tomatoes are not red.	_____	All tomatoes are red.
Tim Couch is a good quarterback.	_____	Tim Couch is not a good quarterback.
No guns are loud.	_____	Some guns are not loud.
Some rocks are crystals.	_____	Some rocks are not crystals.
Some men are sinners.	_____	Some men are not sinners.
No men are saved.	_____	Some men are not saved.
All wars are bloody.	_____	No wars are bloody.
Some soldiers are not brave.	_____	All soldiers are brave.
Some animals are amphibian.	_____	No animals are amphibian.
No houses are well-built.	_____	All houses are well-built.
All storms are violent.	_____	Some storms are violent.
All machines are loud.	_____	Some machines are loud.

14. Explain why the A statement "All S is P" and the E statement "No S is P" are not subcontrary.

_____ Exercises for Day 3. **Read "The Rule of Subalterns." Read it carefully.**

15. Express the Rule of Subalterns.

16. Tell the quality and quantity of the A statement.

17. Tell the quality and quantity of the I statement.

18. Is the A statement subalternate to the I statement? If so, explain why; if not, explain why not.

19. Are there any other pairs of statements that are subalternate to one another? If so, indicate which they are.

20. Indicate which of the following pairs of statements are subalternate to one another by writing an *S* between each pair of subalternate statements:

All logic problems are difficult.	_____	Some logic problems are difficult.
No logic problems are difficult.	_____	All logic problems are difficult.
Some logic problems are difficult.	_____	No logic problems are difficult.
Some logic problems are not difficult.	_____	All logic problems are difficult.
All logic problems are difficult.	_____	No logic problems are difficult.
No logic problems are difficult.	_____	Some logic problems are not difficult.
Some logic problems are difficult.	_____	Some logic problems are not difficult.
Some men are white.	_____	Some men are not white.
No men are white.	_____	Some men are not white.
All men are white.	_____	No men are white.
Some men are not white.	_____	All men are white.
Some men are white.	_____	No men are white.
No men are white.	_____	All men are white.
All men are white.	_____	Some men are white.

Read "The Fourth Law of Opposition." Read it carefully.

21. What is the Fourth Law of Opposition?

22. Which pairs of statements comply with the Fourth Law of Opposition?

23. Can both A and I statements be true at the same time?

24. Can both A and I statements be false at the same time?

25. Can both E and O statements be true at the same time?

26. Can both E and O statements be false at the same time?

27. Indicate which of the following pairs of statements are subalternate by writing an *S* between each pair of subalternate statements:

No cars are fast.	_____ All cars are fast.
Some omelettes are tasty.	_____ No omelettes are tasty.
Some tomatoes are not red.	_____ All tomatoes are red.
Michael Jordan is a good basketball player.	_____ Michael Jordan is not a good basketball player.
No guns are loud.	_____ Some guns are not loud.
Some rocks are crystals.	_____ Some rocks are not crystals.
Some men are sinners.	_____ Some men are not sinners.
No men are saved.	_____ Some men are not saved.
All wars are bloody.	_____ No wars are bloody.
Some soldiers are not brave.	_____ All soldiers are brave.
Some animals are amphibian.	_____ No animals are amphibian.
No houses are well-built.	_____ All houses are well-built.
All storms are violent.	_____ Some storms are violent.
All machines are loud.	_____ Some machines are loud.

28. Explain why the A statement "All S is P" and the E statement "No S is P" are not subalternate.

29. Explain why the I statement "Some S is P" and the O statement "Some S is not P" are not subalternate.

Exercises for Day 4. **Read "Summary." Read the entire section carefully.**

30. Fill out the following chart:

		___________	
		Affirmative	Negative
	Universal	_____	_____
_________			
	Particular	_____	_____

31. In the following chart, indicate, as in Figure 7-2, which two pairs of statements are contradictory which two statements are contrary, which two statements are subcontrary, and which two statements are subalternate:

A	E
I	O

32. Write five pairs of subcontrary statements that are not in the book.

33. Write five pairs of subalternate statements that are not in the book.

34. Indicate whether the following statements are true or false:

T	F	Two statements are subcontrary if they differ from each other in quality, and are both particular.
T	F	The quality of the statement "All S is P" is universal.
T	F	The quantity of the statement "Some S is P" is particular.
T	F	The A statement and the I statement differ in quality and quantity.
T	F	The statements "All S is P" and "Some S is P" can both be true at the same time.
T	F	The statements "All S is P" and "Some S is P" can both be false at the same time.
T	F	The A statement and the E statement are not subcontrary because, although they differ in quality, they are both universal.
T	F	The statement "Just do it" and the statement "All men are mortal" are subcontrary.
T	F	The statements "All football players are big" and "Some football players are big" are subalternate.
T	F	Subalternate statements cannot at the same time be false, but they can both be true.

Review Exercises for Day 4.

35. What is the First Law of Opposition?

36. What is the Second Law of Opposition?

37. Can both A and O statements be true at the same time?

38. Can both A and O statements be false at the same time?

39. Can both E and I statements be true at the same time?

40. Can both E and I statements be false at the same time?

41. Can both A and E statements be true at the same time?

42. Can both A and E statements be false at the same time?

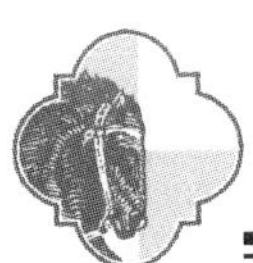

Distribution of Terms

Introduction. In the last two chapters, we studied the ways in which propositions are different from (or *opposed to*) one another; in other words, how these propositions are logically different. In the next chapter, we will discuss the different ways in which they are equivalent to one another—in other words, the ways in which they are logically the same. But before we discuss in what ways statements are equivalent, we need to familiarize ourselves with what is called ***distribution***.

What is Distribution? Distribution may be defined as follows:

Distribution is the status of a term in regard to its extension.

Distribution is the status of a term in regard to its extension.

All of the categorical statements we have learned about (A, I, E, and O) have a subject. The subject of a statement is the term the statement is about. In the statement "All S is P," S is the subject. In the statement "All men are mortal," 'men' is the subject.

In addition, all of the statements we have learned about have a predicate. A predicate is the term we use to say something about the subject. In the statement "All S is P," P is the predicate. In the statement "All men are mortal," 'mortal' is the predicate.

We will be asking whether the terms used as subject and predicate in each one of the four statements we have learned are ***distributed*** or not. When we say that a term is distributed, we mean that the term refers to all the members of the class of things denoted by the term. When we use the term 'man' in a statement, for example, are we referring to it universally—in other words, are we referring to all men? Or are we referring to it particularly—are we referring to only some men? If we are using it universally, we say it is distributed.

When we use the term 'mortal' in a statement, are we using it universally—are we referring to all mortal things? Or are we using it particularly—are we referring only to some mortal things?

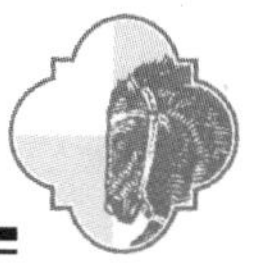

The subject-term is distributed in statements whose quantity is universal and undistributed in statements whose quantity is particular.

We say that a term is distributed when it is used universally—if it refers to all the members of the class denoted by the term. If it is used particularly—if it only refers to some members of the class denoted by the term—then we say it is ***undistributed***.

__________ **Distribution of the Subject-Term.** It is fairly easy to determine whether the subject-term is distributed. The rule for determining the distribution of the subject-term is as follows:

> ***The subject-term is distributed in statements whose quantity is universal and undistributed in statements whose quantity is particular.***

Determining the distribution of the subject-term is easy because the quantifier ('All,' 'Some,' 'No,' and 'Some ... not') tells us all we need to know. If it says, "All S is P," we know it refers to *all* S's. It refers to all the members of the class it denotes. If we say, "All men are mortal," we know it means *all* men. It refers to all the members of the class it denotes. A subject-term in an A statement, then, is taken universally, and is therefore distributed.

The same goes for the E statement. It says, "No S is P." To how many members of the class denoted by S does this E statement refer? To all of them. To say, "No S is P" is the same as saying, "All S is not P." In other words, the subject-term of the E statement is taken universally and is therefore distributed.

Likewise, when we say, "Some S is P," we are obviously not referring to all S's, only some of them. And when we say, "Some men are mortal," we are referring only to some men, not all of them. In both of these cases, the subject-terms are undistributed.

The O statement too, "Some S is not P," obviously has a subject term that is not universal and therefore is undistributed.

In the case of the subject-term, the quantifier tells us all we need to know.

We can see how distribution works with the subject-term in the following diagram:

DIAGRAM OF THE DISTRIBUTION OF TERMS IN A, I, E, AND O STATEMENTS

Type of sentence	Subject-Term
A	Distributed
I	Undistributed
E	Distributed
O	Undistributed

In affirmative propositions the predicate-term is always undistributed, and in negative propositions,the predicate is always taken universally.

__________**Distribution of the Predicate-Term.** The rule for determining the distribution of the predicate-term is not quite as straightforward as for the subject:

> ***In affirmative propositions the predicate-term is always taken particularly (and therefore undistributed), and in negative propositions the predicate is always taken universally (and therefore distributed).***

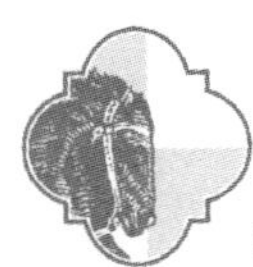

Distribution of the Predicate-Term in A Statements: Let us take A statements first. When we say, "All S is P," is P taken universally? Are we talking about all P's? To make it a little clearer, let's take a real statement. When we say, "All men are animals," we know we are talking about all men: the sentence says so quite plainly. But are we talking about all animals? We know, if the statement is true, that all men are animals, but are all animals men? Obviously not. Although the statement is about all men, it is only about those animals who are men. We are talking about all men, but only some animals, since only some animals are men. The predicate-term is therefore taken particularly, and is therefore undistributed.

We can use a diagram invented by a Swiss mathematician named Euler to visually show how this works. In Euler's diagram (see Diagram 8-1 to the left), we represent each term, 'man' and 'animal,' by a circle. Remember in Chapter 2, when we were discussing extension, that we concluded that the concept 'animal' had greater extension than the concept 'man.' Man was only one of many kinds of animals. Using Euler's diagram, we show a concept with greater extension with a larger circle than a concept with lesser extension.

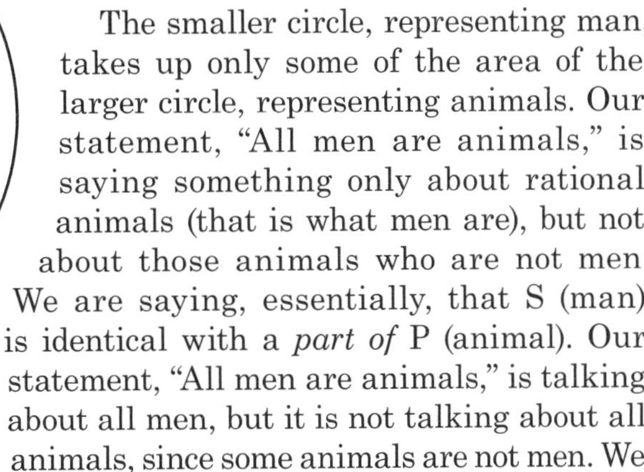

DIAGRAM 8-1

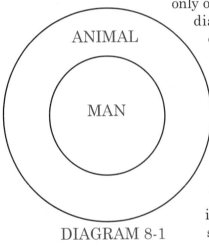

The smaller circle, representing man, takes up only some of the area of the larger circle, representing animals. Our statement, "All men are animals," is saying something only about rational animals (that is what men are), but not about those animals who are not men. We are saying, essentially, that S (man) is identical with a *part of* P (animal). Our statement, "All men are animals," is talking about all men, but it is not talking about all animals, since some animals are not men. We say, therefore, that although 'man' is distributed, 'animal' is not.

In A statements, the predicate-term is undistributed.

In A statements, then, the predicate-term is undistributed.

Distribution of the Predicate-Term in I Statements: In I statements, "Some S is P," we can also see that not only are we talking about some S's, but we are also only talking about some P's. When we say, "Some dogs are vicious things," we are only talking about some dogs, not all, and some vicious things (the ones that are dogs), not all vicious things. There are other dogs that are not vicious. And there are other vicious things (wolverines, tasmanian devils, etc.) that are not dogs. Euler would show this as in Diagram 8-2 on the next page.

Here you see a shaded area which represents what the I statement, "Some dogs are vicious things," is referring to. As you can see, the shaded area does not take up all the circle representing dogs, nor does it take up all the area of the circle representing vicious things. It is saying that 'some dogs' (the ones in the shaded area) are 'vicious things' (the ones in the shaded area). And we are talking about only some vicious things as well. The predicate, 'vicious things,' is particular and therefore undistributed.

The predicate-term in I statements is undistributed.

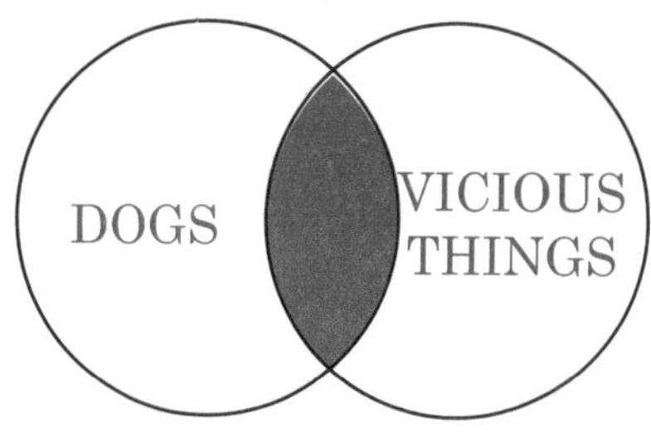

DIAGRAM 8-2

Distribution of the Predicate-Term in E Statements: As in A statements, the subject of an E statement is universal and therefore is distributed. But what about the predicate? When we say, "No man is a reptile," we are, in fact, talking about all men. We are saying that "All men are not reptiles." But are we saying something about all reptiles? Can we infer from the statement "No man is a reptile" that "All reptiles are not men"? We certainly can. We *are* talking about all reptiles. We are taking reptiles universally, and therefore it is distributed.

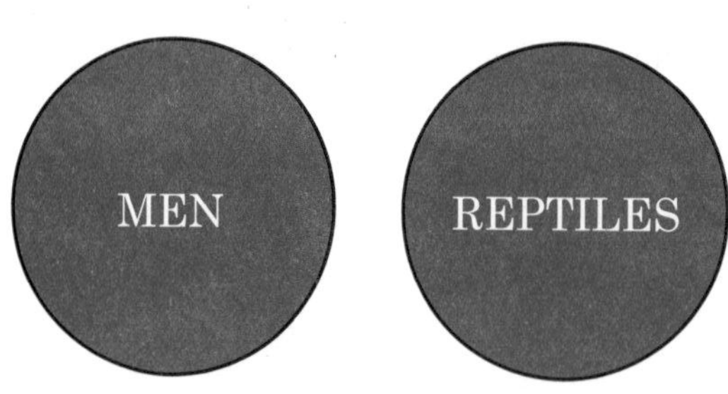

DIAGRAM 8-3

You can see this in Diagram 8-3 to the left.

As you can see, the circles do not overlap at all. This illustrates the fact that no men are reptiles. There are men and there are reptiles, but there is nothing in this world that is both: there are no 'reptile-men.' They are two completely different things, represented by two circles that do not overlap.

The predicate-term in O statements is distributed.

Distribution of the Predicate-Term in O Statements: When we look at the O statement, "Some S is not P," we see that the subject-term is not distributed (we are only talking about *some*, not *all*, S's.) But what about P's? If we said, for example, "Some men are not blind," we know we can't say that all men are not blind (only some of them are not blind.) But these 'some men' who are 'not blind'—are they excluded from only part of the class of blind things or are they excluded from the entire class? The some men who are not blind are, of course, excluded from the whole class of blind things. Therefore, in the O statement we are taking P universally. It is therefore distributed.

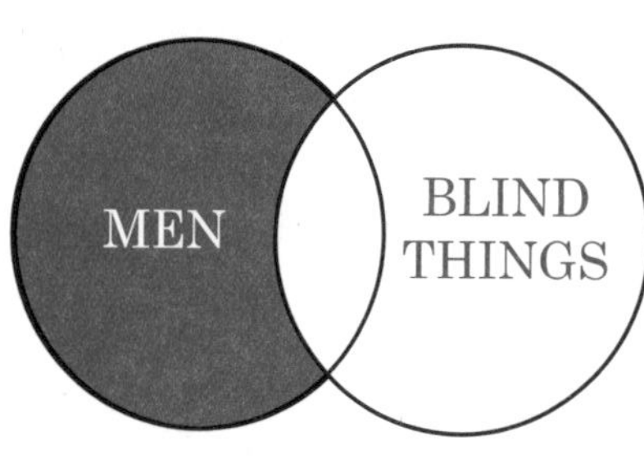

DIAGRAM 8-4

In Diagram 8-4 to the left, you see that although the darkened part of the circle represents 'some men,' it obviously does not represent all men, and is therefore undistributed. But the predicate represents the whole circle which represents all blind things and is therefore distributed.

We know, then, that in E and O statements the predicate is distributed. But in A and I statements the predicate is undistributed. Let us then reformulate our diagram to

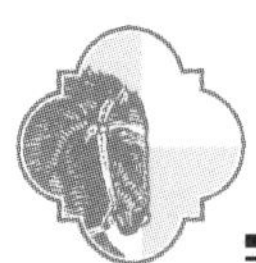

show the distribution of both the subject and the predicate in all four of our categorical statements:

DIAGRAM OF THE DISTRIBUTION OF TERMS IN A, I, E, AND O STATEMENTS

Type of sentence	Subject-Term	Predicate-Term
A	Distributed	Undistributed
I	Undistributed	Undistributed
E	Distributed	Distributed
O	Undistributed	Distributed

__________ **Different Ways to Diagram I and O Statements.** When we discussed distribution in I and O statements earlier in this chapter, we left a few things out. When we discussed I statements, for example, we used this statement to illustrate distribution: "Some dogs are vicious things." And we illustrated this with a diagram like 8-5 below (which is the same as 8-2):

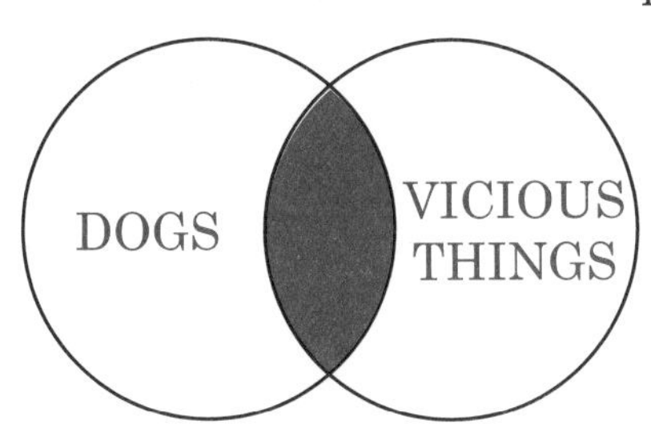

DIAGRAM 8-5

But what we didn't mention when we were discussing this statement is that there are other kinds of I statements that require another kind of diagram.

There is another kind of I statement that requires another kind of diagram.

Let's take, for example, the following statement:

Some men are carpenters.

This is different from the first I statement we looked at for this reason: Although there are some vicious things that are not dogs, there are no carpenters who are not men. This means that we need another kind of diagram to represent this statement.

MEN
CARPEN-TERS

DIAGRAM 8-6

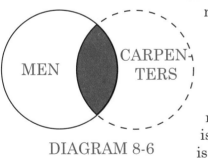

To represent an I statement like "Some men are carpenters," we will need Diagram 8-6. The broken lines of the circle representing carpenters indicates that there is nothing in that part of the circle. This is a visual way of saying that there are no carpenters who are not men. Not all men are carpenters: only some of them are. But all carpenters are men.

The same goes for O statements. We used the example, "Some men are not blind." We know that there are some creatures besides men who are blind. Some kinds of cave-dwelling creatures, for example, are blind. So we used a diagram like that in Diagram 8-7 on the next page.

But what if we used the example "Some men are not carpenters"? In this case, we would have to use a different diagram altogether. It would have to look like Diagram 8-8 on the next page.

If there is any member of the predicate class in an I statement that is not a member of the subject class, then you use the diagram with the solid line. If not, then you use the broken line.

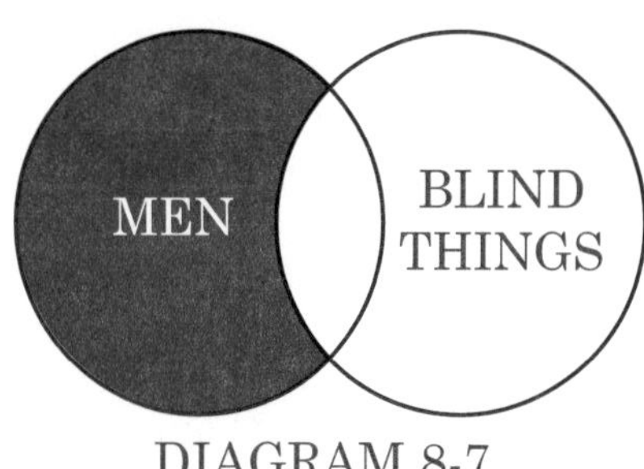

DIAGRAM 8-7

Here we see a broken line on the white circle that we do not see in Diagram 8-7. This is because, although there are some blind things that are not men, there are no carpenters who are not men. We used a broken line to indicate that there are no carpenters outside the class of men.

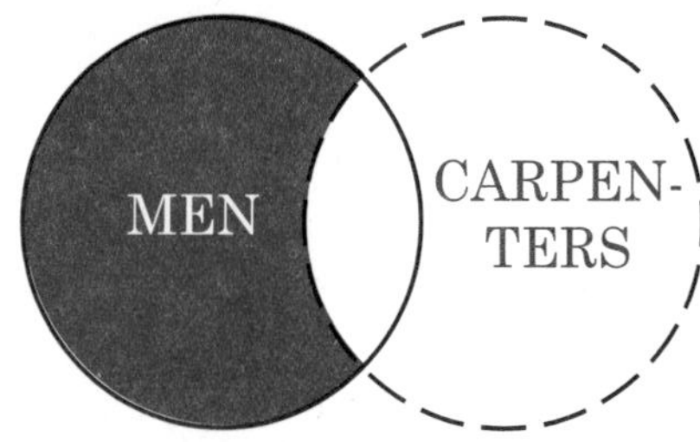

DIAGRAM 8-8

When you are working with I and O statements, you will need to determine which kind they are: Are they like "Some men are not blind"? Or are they like "Some men are not carpenters"? Just ask whether there is any member of the predicate class that is not a member of the subject class. If there is, then you use the diagram with the solid line. If there is not, then you use a diagram with a broken line.

__________ **Summary.** In this chapter, we discuss distribution. ***Distribution*** is the status of a term in regard to its extension. When we say that a term is distributed, we mean that the term refers to all the members of the class of things denoted by the term. We said that the subject-term is distributed in statements whose quantity is universal and undistributed in statements whose quantity is particular. In regard to the predicate-term, we said that in affirmative propositions the predicate-term is always taken particularly (and therefore undistributed), and in negative propositions the predicate is always taken universally (and therefore distributed).

We showed how distribution works with both subject and predicate terms by using the following diagram:

The predicate-term in O statements is distributed.

DIAGRAM OF THE DISTRIBUTION OF TERMS IN A, I, E, AND O STATEMENTS

Type of sentence	Subject-Term	Predicate-Term
A	Distributed	Undistributed
I	Undistributed	Undistributed
E	Distributed	Distributed
O	Undistributed	Distributed

Finally, we showed how to use diagrams to display the distribution of various categorical statements.

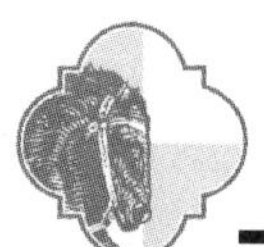

_____________ **Exercises for Day 1. Peruse the entire chapter. Then read the introductory section at the very beginning of Chapter 8. Read this section carefully and try to understand it as best you can.**

1. What are we discussing in this chapter?

2. What is the definition of 'distribution'?

3. What is a subject?

4. In the statement "All men are mortal," what is the subject?

5. In the statement "All men are mortal," what is the predicate?

6. When we say that a term is distributed, what do we mean?

7. When a term is used universally, is it distributed or undistributed?

8. When a term is used particularly, is it distributed or undistributed?

_____________ **Exercises for Day 2. Read "Distribution of the Subject-Term." Read it carefully.**

9. What is the rule for determining the distribution of the subject-term?

10. Why is it easy to determine if the subject term is distributed?

11. In the A statement, "All S is P," is the subject-term distributed or undistributed?

12. In the E statement, "No S is P," is the subject-term distributed or undistributed?

13. In the I statement, "Some S is P," is the subject-term distributed or undistributed?

14. In the O statement, "Some S is not P," is the subject-term distributed or undistributed?

15. In determining whether the subject-term is distributed or undistributed the ____________________ tell us all we need to know.

16. Fill out the following diagram:

DIAGRAM OF THE DISTRIBUTION OF TERMS IN A, I, E, AND O STATEMENTS

Type of sentence	Subject-Term
A	____________________
I	____________________
E	____________________
O	____________________

17. Tell whether the subjects in the following statements are distributed or undistributed:

All logic problems are difficult.	No men are white.
No logic problems are difficult.	All men are white.
Some logic problems are difficult.	Some men are not white.
Some logic problems are not difficult.	Some men are white.
All logic problems are difficult.	No men are white.
No logic problems are difficult.	All men are white.

________ Exercises for Day 3. Read "Distribution of the Predicate-Term." Read it carefully.

18. What is the rule for determining the distribution of the predicate-term?

19. In the A statement, "All S is P," is the predicate-term distributed or undistributed?

20. In the E statement, "No S is P," is the predicate-term distributed or undistributed?

21. In the I statement, "Some S is P," is the predicate-term distributed or undistributed?

22. In the O statement, "Some S is not P," is the predicate-term distributed or undistributed?

23. Draw a Euler's diagram of this statement: "All ducks are birds."

24. Draw a Euler's diagram of this statement: "Some ducks are white."

25. Draw a Euler's diagram of this statement: "No ducks are criminals."

26. Draw a Euler's diagram of this statement: "Some ducks are not white."

27. Fill out the following diagram:

DIAGRAM OF THE DISTRIBUTION OF TERMS IN A, I, E, AND O STATEMENTS

Type of sentence	Subject-Term	Predicate-Term
A	__________________	__________________
I	__________________	__________________
E	__________________	__________________
O	__________________	__________________

28. Indicate whether the subject-terms and the predicate-terms in the following statements are distributed or undistributed (D=distributed; UnD=undistributed):

No cars are fast.	S:	D	UnD	P:	D	UnD
Some omelettes are tasty.	S:	D	UnD	P:	D	UnD
Some tomatoes are not red.	S:	D	UnD	P:	D	UnD
Michael Jordan is a good basketball player.	S:	D	UnD	P:	D	UnD
No guns are loud.	S:	D	UnD	P:	D	UnD
Some rocks are crystals.	S:	D	UnD	P:	D	UnD
Some men are sinners.	S:	D	UnD	P:	D	UnD

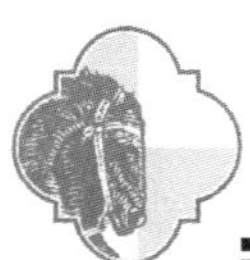

No men are saved.	S:	D	UnD	P:	D	UnD
All wars are bloody.	S:	D	UnD	P:	D	UnD
Some soldiers are not brave.	S:	D	UnD	P:	D	UnD
Some animals are amphibians.	S:	D	UnD	P:	D	UnD
No houses are well-built.	S:	D	UnD	P:	D	UnD
All storms are violent.	S:	D	UnD	P:	D	UnD
All machines are loud.	S:	D	UnD	P:	D	UnD

__________ **Exercises for Day 4.** **Read "Different Ways to Diagram I and O Statements." Read it carefully.**

29. In what way is the I statement "Some dogs are vicious" different from the I statement "Some men are carpenters"?

30. In what way is the O statement "Some men are not blind" different from the O statement "Some men are not carpenters"?

31. Draw a Euler's diagram representing the statement "Some boys are boy scouts."

32. Draw a Euler's diagram representing the statement "Some boys are fast."

33. Draw a Euler's diagram representing the statement "Some boys are not Boy Scouts."

34. Draw a Euler's diagram representing the statement "Some boys are not fast."

35. Write the statement represented by the following Euler's diagram:

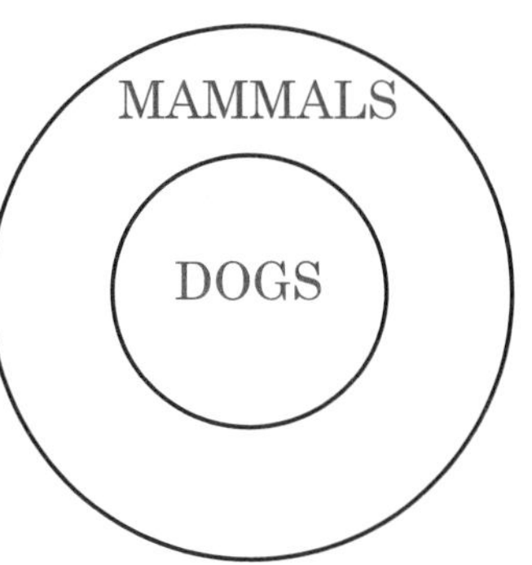

36. Write the statement represented by the following diagram:

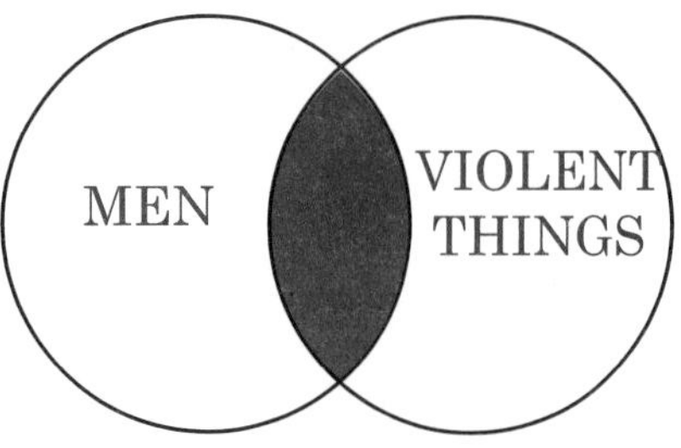

37. Write the statement represented by the following diagram:

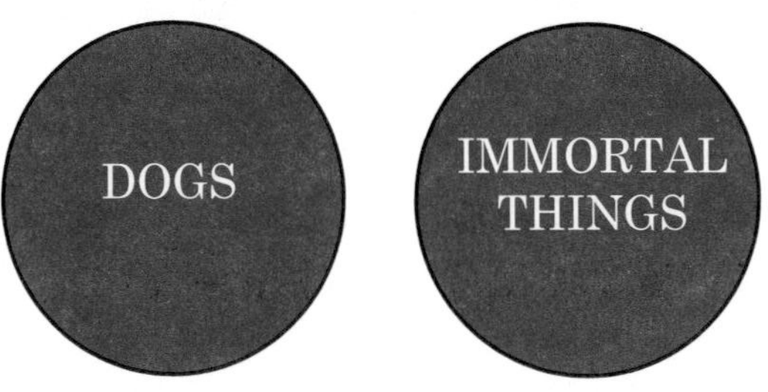

38. Write the statement represented by the following diagram:

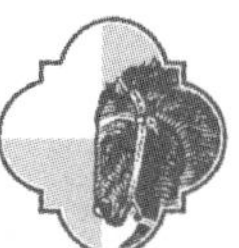

39. Indicate whether the following statements are true or false:

T	F	The subject-term is distributed in statements whose quantity is universal.
T	F	The subject-term is undistributed in statements whose quantity is universal.
T	F	The subject-term in the I statement is undistributed.
T	F	The subject-term in the E statement is undistributed.
T	F	In affirmative propositions the predicate-term is always taken universally.
T	F	In negative propositions, the predicate is always taken universally.

________ Review Exercises for Day 4.

40. Fill out the following chart. [Review]

		________	
		Affirmative	Negative
	Universal	_____	_____
________			
	Particular	_____	_____

41. In the following chart, indicate, as in Figure 6-2, which two pairs of statements are contradictory, which two statements are contrary, which two statements are subcontrary and which two pairs of statements are subalternate. [Review]

A	E
I	O

42. Indicate whether the following statements are true or false:

T	F	The A statement and the E statement are not subcontrary because, although they differ in quality, they do not differ in quantity.
T	F	The statement "Just do it" and the statement "All men are mortal" are subcontrary.
T	F	The statements "All football players are big" and "Some football players are big" are subalternate.
T	F	Subalternate statements cannot at the same time be false, but they can both be true.

Obversion, Conversion, and Contraposition

Introduction. In Chapter 6 we said that there were two kinds of relationships among categorical propositions: relationships of opposition and relationships of equivalence. In Chapters 6 and 7 we studied the ways in which propositions are opposed to one another. In this chapter, we will discuss the different ways in which propositions are equivalent.

In logic, the way we say two statements are logically the same (even though they may use slightly different words) is by calling them ***logically equivalent***. Equivalent propositions can be converted into each other in various ways.

There are three ways to convert propositions into their logical equivalents:

Obversion
Conversion
Contraposition

There are three ways to convert propositions into their logical equivalents: obversion, conversion, and contraposition.

Obversion. To obvert a sentence, you must do two things:

1. Change the quality of the sentence.
2. Negate the predicate.

To change the quality is easy: if the statement is affirmative, you simply make it negative. If the statement is negative, you simply make it affirmative. But be careful. Do not change the quantity of the statement. For example, if you say, "All S is P," you change it to "No S is P." Do not change it to "Some S is not P." If you did the latter, you would be changing the quality, but you would also be changing the quantity, which is not allowed.

Here are a few examples of how this first step works:

All S is P ----------------> No S is P
No S is P ----------------> All S is P
Some S is P ---------------> Some S is not P
Some S is not P -------------> Some S is P

To obvert a sentence, you must do two things: change the quality of the statement and negate the predicate.

To negate the predicate is also easy: you simply place a ***not*** in front of it. If you say, for example, "All S is P," and, in accordance with step 1, change the quality, you get "No S is P." Negating the predicate, as step 2 requires, would yield "No S is not P."

Obversion, unlike conversion and contraposition, works on all four kinds of propositions, A, I, E, and O. In other words, if we obvert any of these four statements, we will get a statement that is logically equivalent to the original.

Once we have applied both step 1 and step 2, we end up with statements that do not look as if they mean the same thing, but they are in fact logically equivalent.

Let's look at the statements we started out with and see what they look like after both steps 1 and 2 have been applied:

All S is P -----------------> No S is not P
No S is P -----------------> All S is not P
Some S is P -----------------> Some S is not non-P
Some S is not P ---------> Some S is not P

If, for example, we want to obvert "All men are mortal," we say, "No men are not mortal." Logically, they mean the same thing. And if we want to obvert "No men are gods," we say, "All men are not gods." Again, they mean the same thing for the purposes of logic.

Notice that with the I statement, you get two negations in the predicate after you obvert.

___________ **Double Negation of the Predicate in I Statements.** Let's take a close look at the I statement for a moment. Notice that with the I statement, you get two negations in the predicate after you obvert: "Some S is P" gets turned into "Some S is not non-P." This is because, under step 1 of obversion, you have changed the quality from affirmative to negative (which in particular statements you perform by negating the predicate), and then under step 2, you negate the predicate. In other words, you end up negating the predicate twice.

You can handle this in any one of four different ways: first, you can simply have two 'not's in the statement, right next to each other. Secondly, you can make the 'not' directly in front of the predicate (i.e., the second 'not') a 'non,' which means the same thing, but can sometimes sound better. Thirdly, you can incorporate the second negation in the predicate word itself by placing an 'im,' an 'un,' an 'in,' or an 'ir' at the beginning of the word you are using in the predicate. For example, if the original predicate was 'mortal,' you could take care of the second negation by using the word 'immortal.' (Be careful with this method, however, since there are some words which, when 'im,' 'un,' 'in,' or 'ir' are placed at the beginning of the word, are not the actual negation of the original word.) Finally, you can apply the rule of double negation (see discussion in the following paragraphs).

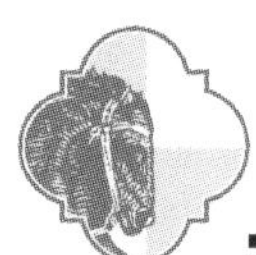

FOUR WAYS OF PHRASING THE PREDICATE WHEN OBVERTING I STATEMENTS

1. Simply place two 'not's at the beginning of the predicate-term.
2. Make the second 'not' a 'non' and attach it to the predicate word with a dash.
3. Place an 'im,' 'un,' 'in,' or an 'ir' at the beginning of the predicate-term.
4. Apply the rule of double negation.

Be careful that you do not negate the predicate-term by using an antonym. An antonym is a word which has a definition that is opposite that of another word. For example, if the predicate-term is 'large,' do not negate it by using the word 'small.' The negation of the thing to which the predicate refers may not be either large or small, but somewhere in between.

Again, obversion works on all four kinds of propositions.

__________ **Double Negation.** How do you apply step 2, which involves putting a 'not' in front of the predicate, if there is already a 'not' there? You can apply one of the first three ways of negating the predicate of an I statement, but sometimes this can sound rather awkward. For example, obverting "Some men have brown hair" to "Some men do not have non-brown hair" simply doesn't sound right.

The solution to this difficulty lies in applying the logical rule of ***double negation***.

The rule of double negation says that a term which is not negated is equivalent to a term that is negated twice (and vice-versa).

The rule of double negation says that a term which is not negated is equivalent to a term that is negated twice (and vice versa).

In other words, "not not P" is logically equivalent to "P." In short, they have exactly the same logical meaning.

In O statements, if we do not apply double negation, we would end up with a triple negation, "Some S is not not not P." We can get rid of two 'not's by applying double negation, yielding, "Some S is not P," which, of course, is the same statement with which you began. In regard to O statements, then, it is best just to remember that the obverse of an O statement is the same as the original O statement. In other words, in practical terms it really doesn't change at all.

We do not always need to apply the rule of double negation, but we can. There are times when applying double negation sounds awkward. In cases such as this, we do not need to use the rule.

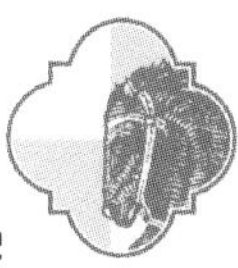

_________ **Conversion.** Conversion is even easier than obversion, since it involves only one step. It is as follows:

> Interchange the subject and predicate.

To convert E and I statements, simply interchange the subject and predicate.

Here are the ways in which sentences are converted:

No S is P	------------>	No P is S
Some S is P	----------->	Some P is S

Notice that we have converted only the E statement and the I statement. That is because conversion only yields a logically equivalent statement with these two kinds of statements. Conversion, in other words, does not work with A and O statements.

We can convert "No men are gods" and get "No gods are men." And we can convert "Some men have brown hair" and get "Some things that have brown hair are men." In both of these cases we get a logically equivalent sentence as a result. But if we try to convert "All men are animals," we get "All animals are men." But these two statements are obviously not logically equivalent. And if we convert "Some men are not accountants," we get "Some accountants are not men." These are obviously not logically equivalent.

Partial Conversion of the A Statement: We should add that A statements can be partially converted. If an A statement is true, it can be converted into a true I statement, but it must be done in a slightly different way.

Partial conversion of the A statement is done by interchanging the subject and predicate and changing the statement from universal to particular.

The partial conversion of A can be accomplished by interchanging the subject and the predicate just as in ordinary conversion, but also changing the quantity. If we say "All dogs are animals," we cannot do a normal conversion and say "All animals are dogs." But we can do a partial conversion resulting in "Some animals are dogs."

We need to think about this only briefly to see the sense of it. If, for example, all men are mortal, doesn't that imply that some mortals are men? If all the members of your family are eating dinner, are not at least some of the people eating dinner members of your family?

Again, partial conversion of the A statement is done by interchanging the subject and predicate and changing the statement from universal to particular.

_________ **Contraposition.** Contraposition, the third method of converting statements into their equivalents, is accomplished in three steps:

1. Obvert the statement.
2. Convert the statement.
3. Obvert the statement again.

Only the A and O statements can be converted in this way. It is not to be used with I and E statements (E statements can be partially converted, but we will not discuss that here.)

Here is an example of how to contrapose an A statement:

Original sentence: All men are mortal

Step 1, Obvert:	No men are non-mortal
Step 2, Convert:	No non-mortals are men
Step 3, Obvert:	All non-mortals are non-men

As we mentioned, this can also be done with O statements. Here are the ways in which statements may be contraposed:

All S is P	----------------->	All non-P is non-S
Some S is not P	--------------->	Some non-P is S

Contraposition of A and O statements involves three steps: obvert, convert, and obvert again.

____________ **Summary.** There are three ways statements can be converted into their logical equivalents: obversion, conversion, and contraposition.

An A statement can be obverted by 1) changing its quality and 2) negating the predicate. ***Obversion*** is permissible with all four kinds of statements.

A statement can be converted by simply interchanging the subject and predicate. ***Conversion*** works only for E and I statements, although true A statements can be partially converted into true I statements.

Contraposition is accomplished by first obverting the statement, then converting, and then obverting the statement again. Contraposition may be used only with A and O statements.

____________ **Review of Chapters 4-9.** In Chapter 4 we moved from the study of ***simple apprehension*** (the subject of Chapters 1-3) to the study of judgment. We said that ***judgment*** is a mental act whose verbal expression is what we call a ***proposition***. We said that judgment can be defined as the act by which the intellect unites by affirming, or separates by denying. A proposition is a sentence or statement which expresses truth or falsity. The three elements of any proposition are the subject-term, the predicate-term, and the copula. Finally, sentences are much more easily handled in logic if they are put into proper ***logical form***, which means that they must show all three elements of a logical proposition clearly.

In Chapter 5 we said first that there are four basic categorical propositions with which formal logic deals: "All S is P"; "Some S is P"; "No S is P"; and "Some S is not P." We noted that, in addition to the three components, the subject-term (S), the predicate-term (P), and the copula (is), there is a fourth component: the quantifier. The quantifiers are the words 'All,' 'Some,' 'No,' and 'Some ... not.'

We said that there are two fundamental characteristics of categorical propositions: quality and quantity. ***Quality*** has to do with whether astatement is affirmative or negative. ***Quantity*** has to do with whether a proposition is universal or particular.

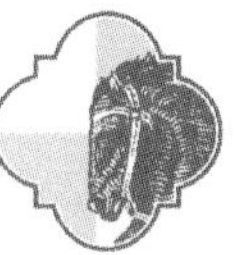

We can summarize the quality and quantity of each statement as follows:

A: Affirmative-Universal
I: Affirmative-Particular
E: Negative-Universal
O: Negative-Particular

See Figure 5-1 for a diagram of these characteristics of categorical propositions.

In Chapters 6-7 we learned that, according to the ***Rule of Contradiction***, two statements are contradictory if they differ in both quality and quantity. According to the ***First Law of Opposition***, two contradictory statements cannot both be true at the same time, nor can they both be false at the same time.

If you ever get confused about which statements are contradictory, contrary, subcontrary, or subalternate, all you have to do is consult Figure 7-2.

We also learned in Chapter 6 that, according to the ***Rule of Contraries***, two statements are contrary if they are both universal but differ in quality. According to the ***Second Law of Opposition***, two contraries cannot at the same time both be true, but can at the same time both be false.

According to the ***Rule of Subcontraries***, two statements are subcontrary if they are both particular statements that differ in quality. According to the ***Third Law of Opposition***, two subcontraries may at the same time be true, but cannot at the same time be false.

We also learned in Chapter 8 that, according to the ***Rule of Subalterns***, two statements are subalternate if they have the same quality, but differ in quantity. According to the ***Fourth Law of Opposition***, subalterns may both be true or both be false. If the particular is false, the universal is false; if the universal is true, then the particular is true; otherwise their status is indeterminate.

If you ever get confused about which statements are contradictory, contrary, subcontrary, or subalternate, all you have to do is consult Figure 7-2, where all the relationships are visually illustrated.

In Chapter 8 we discussed distribution. ***Distribution*** is the status of a term in regard to its extension. When we say that a term is distributed, we mean that the term refers to all the members of the class of things denoted by the term.

We showed how distribution works with both subject and predicate terms by using the following diagram:

DIAGRAM OF THE DISTRIBUTION OF TERMS IN A, I, E, AND O STATEMENTS

Type of sentence	Subject-Term	Predicate-Term
A	Distributed	Undistributed
I	Undistributed	Undistributed
E	Distributed	Distributed
O	Undistributed	Distributed

In summary, in Chapter 4 we defined what judgment was and how a proposition (the verbal expression of a judgment) is constructed. In Chapter 5 we dealt with the four logical statements and their quality and quantity. In Chapters 6-7 we talked about the ways in which propositions can be logically opposed to one another. In Chapter 8 we discussed the distribution of terms. And in Chapter 9 we talked about the ways in which propositions can be logically equivalent.

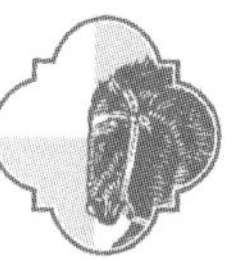

_____________ **Exercises for Day 1. Peruse the entire chapter. Then read the introductory section at the very beginning of Chapter 9. Read this section carefully and try to understand it as best you can.**

1. What are we discussing in this chapter?

2. What phrase do we use to indicate that two statements are logically the same?

3. What are the three ways in which statements can be converted into their logical equivalents?

Read "Obversion." Read it carefully.

4. Give the two-step method for obverting a statement.

5. How do you change the quality of a statement?

6. Change the quality of the following statements:

   All logic problems are difficult.
   No logic problems are difficult.
   Some logic problems are difficult.
   Some logic problems are not difficult.
   Some men are white.
   All men are white.
   Some men are not white.
   No men are white.

7. How do you negate the predicate of a statement?

8. Negate the predicate in the following statements:

   All logic problems are difficult.
   No logic problems are difficult.
   Some logic problems are difficult.
   Some logic problems are not difficult.
   Some men are white.
   All men are white.
   Some men are not white.
   No men are white.

9. With which of the four categorical statements can obversion be used?

Read "Double Negation of the Predicate in I Statements." Read it carefully.

10. What happens to the predicate in I statements when they are obverted?

11. How does this happen?

12. What are the four ways you can handle the double-negated predicate in an I statement?

13. What do you have to be careful about when using the third of these methods (negating by the use of 'im,' 'un,' 'in,' or 'ir')?

14. Can you negate a predicate-term like 'large' by replacing it with 'small'? If not, explain why.

15. Obvert the following statements. When obverting the I statements, use any one of the first three rules for the double-negated predicates:

 All logic problems are difficult.
 No logic problems are difficult.
 Some logic problems are difficult.
 Some logic problems are not difficult.
 Some men are white.
 All men are white.
 Some men are not white.
 No men are white.

_____________ **Exercises for Day 2.** **Read "Double Negation" and "Conversion." Read them carefully.**

16. What is the rule of double negation?

17. Use the rule of double negation to convert the following terms into another term that is logically equivalent:

not immortal	not non-white
immortal	non-white
mortal	white
not non-immortal	not non-white
logical	not non-animal
illogical	non-animal
not non-illogical	animal
not illogical	not not non-animal

18. When an I statement has been obverted, how many negations are contained in the predicate (before applying the rule of double negation)?

19. When the O statement has been obverted and the rule of double negation applied, to what is the statement similar?

20. When should we apply the rule of double negation and when should we not apply it?

21. How do you convert a statement?

22. Which of the categorical statements (A, E, I, and O) can be converted?

23. Convert the following statements. Write *N/A* if the statement cannot be fully converted into its logical equivalent:

    All logic problems are difficult.
    No logic problems are difficult.
    Some logic problems are difficult.
    Some logic problems are not difficult.
    Some men are white.
    All men are white.
    Some men are not white.
    No men are white.

24. Is there any way in which the A statement can be converted? If so, how?

25. Partially convert the following A statements:

    All mammals breathe oxygen.
    All Americans are brave.
    All pigs are smelly.
    All horses are fast.
    All babies are loud.
    All oysters are quiet.
    All lobsters are angry.
    All geraniums are irrational.

Exercises for Day 3. **Read "Contraposition." Read it carefully.**

26. Give the three-step method for contraposing a statement.

27. Which of the four kinds of categorical statements can be contraposed?

28. Show each step in the process of contraposition for the following statements:

All men are mortal.	Step 1: ____________
	Step 2: ____________
	Step 3: ____________
All men are animals.	Step 1: ____________
	Step 2: ____________
	Step 3: ____________
All pigs are smelly.	Step 1: ____________
	Step 2: ____________
	Step 3: ____________
All oysters are quiet.	Step 1: ____________
	Step 2: ____________
	Step 3: ____________
All lobsters are angry.	Step 1: ____________
	Step 2: ____________
	Step 3: ____________

29. Contrapose the following statements. Write *N/A* if the statement cannot be fully contraposed into its logical equivalent:

    All logic problems are difficult.
    No logic problems are difficult.
    Some logic problems are difficult.
    Some logic problems are not difficult.
    Some men are white.
    All men are white.
    Some men are not white.
    No men are white.

30. Contrapose the following statements. Write *N/A* if the statement cannot be fully contraposed into its logical equivalent:

    No cars are fast.
    Some omelettes are tasty.
    Some tomatoes are not red.
    Michael Jordan is a good basketball player.
    No guns are loud.
    Some rocks are crystals.
    Some men are sinners.
    No men are saved.
    All wars are bloody.
    Some soldiers are not brave.
    Some animals are amphibian.
    No houses are well-built.
    All storms are violent.
    All machines are loud.

______ Exercises for Day 4. **Read "Summary." Read it carefully.**

31. Think of five of your own statements and obvert them.

32. Think of five of your own statements (different from those you used in Question 31) and convert them.

33. Think of five statements (different from those used in Questions 31 and 32) and contrapose them.

34. Each of the statements on the right is logically equivalent to the statement to the left of it. Indicate whether the statement on the right is the obverse, the converse, or the contrapositive of the statement to the left of it (use O for obverse, C for converse, and CP for contrapositive):

All logic problems are difficult.	___	No logic problems are not difficult.
No logic problems are difficult.	___	No difficult things are logic problems.
Some logic problems are difficult.	___	Some difficult things are logic problems.
Some logic problems are not difficult.	___	Some non-difficult things are logic problems.
All logic problems are difficult.	___	All non-difficult things are not logic problems.
No logic problems are difficult.	___	No difficult things are logic problems.
Some logic problems are difficult.	___	Some logic problems are not non-difficult.
Some men are white.	___	Some white people are men.
No men are white.	___	All men are non-white.
All men are white.	___	All non-white things are not men.
Some men are not white.	___	Some non-white people are men.
Some men are white.	___	Some men are not non-white.
No men are white.	___	All men are non-white.
All men are white.	___	All non-white people are non-men.

35. Indicate whether the following statements are true or false:

T	F	The three ways statements can be converted into their logical equivalents are by obversion, conversion, and subalternation.
T	F	Obversion can be performed on all four kinds of statements.
T	F	One of the ways to phrase the predicate when obverting an I statement is to use the rule of double negation.
T	F	Conversion can be performed on O statements.
T	F	A statement can be contraposed by converting it, obverting it, and then converting it again.
T	F	The statement "All lobsters are angry" and the statement "No lobsters are not angry" are contrapositive.
T	F	There are only two steps involved in obversion.

______ Review Exercises for Day 4. **Read "Review of Chapters 4-9." Read it carefully.**

36. Define 'judgment.'

37. Define 'proposition.'

38. What are the four elements of a proposition?

39. What does it mean to say that a proposition is in 'proper logical form'?

40. What are the four basic statements with which logic deals?
(Use the letters S and P to show their form.)

41. What are the two fundamental characteristics of categorical propositions?

42. Show the quality and quantity of the four logical statements by filling out the following chart:

		________	
		Affirmative	Negative
________	Universal	_____	_____
	Particular	_____	_____

43. What is the Rule of Contradiction?

44. What is the Rule of Contraries?

45. What is the Rule of Subcontraries?

46. What is the Rule of Subalternates?

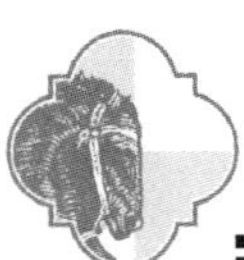

47. In the following chart, indicate, as in Figure 7-2, which two pairs of statements are contradictory, which two statements are contrary, which two statements are subcontrary, and which two pairs of statements are subalternate:

A	E
I	O

48. What is the definition of 'distribution'?

49. Fill out the following diagram:

DIAGRAM OF THE DISTRIBUTION OF TERMS IN A, I, E, AND O STATEMENTS

Type of sentence	Subject-Term	Predicate-Term
A	__________	__________
I	__________	__________
E	__________	__________
O	__________	__________

50. Fill out the following chart showing what was covered in each of the chapters from Chapter 4 through Chapter 9:

Chapter	Topic
Ch. 4:	____________________
Ch. 5:	____________________
Chs. 6-7:	____________________
Ch. 8:	____________________
Ch. 9:	____________________

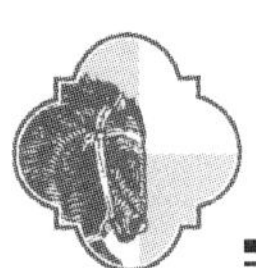

What is Deductive Inference?

Introduction. In the past six chapters, we have discussed ***proposition***, which is the verbal expression of judgment. We discussed how propositions are logically opposed and how they are logically equivalent. We also discussed how terms are distributed in each kind of proposition. In the preceding three chapters, we discussed simple apprehension (or ***term***). Simple apprehension is the first logical operation of the mind; judgment is the second. In this chapter, we will turn to the study of the third logical operation of the mind: syllogism, which is the verbal expression of deductive inference.

Mental Act	Verbal Expression
Simple Apprehension	Term
Judgment	Proposition
Deductive Inference	***Syllogism***

Reasoning is the act by which the mind acquires new knowledge by means of what it already knows.

Reasoning. Deductive inference is one kind of reasoning. Reasoning is defined as follows:

Reasoning is the act by which the mind acquires new knowledge by means of what it already knows.

When we reason, we take truths that are already known to us and, by the use of reasoning, arrive at another truth. There are two kinds of reasoning:

1. Deduction (i.e., Deductive Inference)
2. Induction

Remember that in this book we are studying only deduction.

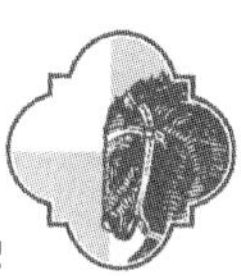

Let us look, once again, at the following argument:

All men are mortal
Socrates is a man
Therefore, Socrates is mortal

Deductive inference is the act by which the mind establishes a connection between the antecedent and the consequent.

There are three acts which occur in our minds when we make an argument like this. First, we perceive the first premise ("All men are mortal") as being true. Secondly, we perceive the second premise ("Socrates is a man") as also true. These two steps are together called the ***antecedent***. The word 'antecedent' is made up of two Latin words: 'ante,' which means 'before,' and 'cedere,' which means 'to go.' These first two steps—the recognition that each of the two premises is true—*go before*, or precede, in the act of reasoning.

Each one of the first two steps is an act of judgment, which is, as we said, the second operation of the mind. The third step is an act of deductive inference, the third logical operation of the mind. This third step takes place when we realize that, given the truth of the two premises ("All men are mortal" and "Socrates is a man"), the conclusion ("Socrates is a mortal") must also be true. Our minds stop, or *conclude*, at this third step, which is why this final statement is called the ***conclusion***. The conclusion is the ***consequent*** in our reasoning.

All men are mortal
Socrates is a man
Therefore, Socrates is mortal

A syllogism is a group of propositions in orderly sequence, one of which (the consequent) is said to be necessarily inferred from the others (the antecedent).

The definition of deductive inference is as follows:

Deductive inference is the act by which the mind establishes a connection between the antecedent and the consequent.

As we have said, deductive inference is the mental act, and it corresponds to the verbal expression we call a ***syllogism***. What is the definition of syllogism?

A syllogism is a group of propositions in orderly sequence, one of which (the consequent) is said to be necessarily inferred from the others (the antecedent).

A syllogism will always contain two premises and a conclusion. The premises are the antecedents and the conclusion is the consequent.

__________ **Validity.** All reasoning presupposes what we may call the ***Essential Law of Argumentation*:**

If the antecedent is true, the consequent must also be true.

All valid syllogisms are governed by this law. A valid syllogism is one which contains a conclusion that logically follows from the premises. We see this law in operation by once again looking at the argument we started out with:

All men are mortal
Socrates is a man
Therefore, Socrates is mortal

We can see that if the antecedent is true (i.e., if both "All men are mortal" and "Socrates is a man" are true), then the statement "Socrates is mortal" must also be true.

This rule has two corollaries to it:

1. If the syllogism is valid and the consequent is false, then the antecedent (i.e., one or both of the two premises) must be false.

2. In a valid syllogism with a true consequent, the antecedent is not necessarily true (i.e., one or both of the premises may still be false).

In a valid argument, if the antecedent is true, the conclusion must also be true.

Let's give an example of corollary 1:

All men are sinners
My dog Spot is a man
Therefore, my dog Spot is a sinner

This syllogism is valid. By saying it is valid, however, we simply mean that if the premises are true, the conclusion must also be true. But the conclusion is false. By applying corollary 1, we see that if the conclusion is false, one or both of the premises must be false. In this particular argument, we see the problem right away: the second premise ("My dog Spot is a man") is obviously false.

Let's also give an illustration of corollary 2:

All vegetables are philosophers
Socrates is a vegetable
Therefore, Socrates is a philosopher

In this syllogism, we notice that the conclusion is true: Socrates was, indeed, a philosopher. But we know from corollary 2 that just because the conclusion is true doesn't mean that the antecedent (i.e., the two premises) must be true. Indeed, we see in this argument that even though the consequent (which we also call the conclusion) is true, neither of the premises are true.

There are three terms in a syllogism: the *major term*, the *minor term*, and the *middle term*.

____________ **Terms in a Syllogism.** There are three terms in a syllogism: the ***major term***, the ***minor term***, and the ***middle term***. They are arrayed in a valid syllogism as follows:

Major term: The major term is the predicate of the conclusion.
Minor term: The minor term is the subject of the conclusion.
Middle term: The middle term is the term that appears in both premises, but not in the conclusion.

Let's look at a real syllogism again:

All men are mortal
Socrates is a man
Therefore, Socrates is mortal

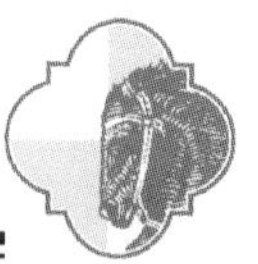

We see in this syllogism that there are six terms used, but some of them are the same. There are actually three terms used twice each. Using the definitions of the three kinds of terms above, we can determine what are the minor, major, and middle terms in this argument.

We see that the minor term is the subject of the conclusion. What is the subject of the conclusion in this argument? It is 'Socrates.' Therefore, 'Socrates' is the minor term.

We see that the predicate of the conclusion is the major term. What is the predicate of the conclusion in the argument? It is 'mortal.' Therefore, 'mortal' is the major term.

We see that the middle term is the term used in both premises, but not in the conclusion. What term in our argument is used in both premises but not in the conclusion? It is 'men.' Therefore, 'men' is the middle term.

We know, then, that the minor term is 'Socrates,' the major term is 'mortal,' and the middle term is 'men.'

One of the premises we call the *major premise* and the other we call the *minor premise*.

Let us now label our terms in order to more easily identify them. Let us label the minor term S, since it is the subject of the conclusion. Let us label the major term P, since it is the predicate of the conclusion. And let us label the middle term M. Our syllogism will then look like this:

> All men^{M} are mortal^{P}
> Socrates^{S} is a man$^{M.}$
> Therefore, Socrates^{S} is mortal^{P}

If we wanted to simplify even further, we could reduce all the terms to letters, just like we did when we were studying statements:

> All M is P
> All S is M
> Therefore, All S is P

In addition to the labels we attach to the terms themselves, there are also labels we attach to the premises in an argument. One of the premises we call the ***major premise***; the other we call the ***minor premise***. How do we know which is which? It is quite simple:

The major premise is the premise which contains the major term.
The minor premise is the premise which contains the minor term.

In our argument, which is the minor and which the major premise?

> All men are mortal
> Socrates is a man
> Therefore, Socrates is mortal

We know that the major term is the predicate of the conclusion. The predicate of the conclusion is 'mortal.' The term 'mortal' is contained in the first premise. Therefore, the first premise is the major premise. We know also that the minor term is the subject of the conclusion. The subject of the conclusion is 'Socrates.' The term 'Socrates' is contained in the second premise. Therefore, the second premise is the minor premise.

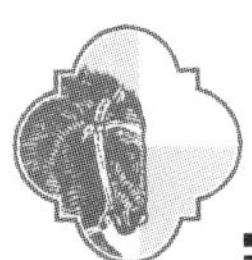

______ **Proper Formation of a Syllogism.** In the example syllogism we just looked at in order to illustrate how to identify the major and minor premises, we found that the major premise was the first one. It is very important to remember that the major premise should always be put first in a syllogism. We say a syllogism is properly formed if the major premise is first, the minor premise second, and the conclusion third.

Note, however, that when we see a syllogism, we should not automatically assume that the first premise is the major premise. The syllogism could be improperly formed and have the minor premise first instead. In that case we should change it so it is properly formed by placing the major premise first. But, in determining which premise is the major premise, do not assume it is the first premise; instead apply the definition of the major premise given above.

The major premise should always be put first in a syllogism.

______ **The Principles of the Syllogism.** Categorical syllogisms state the identity of two terms, the minor and major terms, by virtue of their mutual identity with a third term, the middle term. Behind the rules that govern the syllogism, there are four principles which are fundamental to all logical thought.

The Principle of Reciprocal Identity: ***Two terms that are identical with a third term are identical to each other.*** For example, in the argument above, the term ***mortal*** is said to be identical with the term ***man***; and the term 'mortal' is also said to be identical to the term 'Socrates.' Since both 'Socrates' and 'man' are identical to 'mortal,' then the terms 'Socrates' and 'man' must be identical to each other. In other words, if S is identical with M, and P is identical with M, then S is identical to P.

The Principle of Reciprocal Non-Identity: ***Two terms, one of which is identical with a third term and the other of which is nonidentical with that third term, are nonidentical to each other.*** Consider the following argument:

> No men are angels
> Socrates is a man
> Therefore, Socrates is not an angel

We see here that although 'Socrates' is said to be identical with 'man,' 'angel' is not identical with 'man.' Since 'Socrates' is identical with 'man' but 'angel' is not, 'Socrates' cannot be identical with 'angel.' In other words, if S is identical with M, but P is not identical with M, then S is not identical with P.

The Dictum de Omni: ***What is affirmed universally of a certain term is affirmed of every term that comes under that term.*** This principle is apparent also in our original syllogism. Since mortality is affirmed universally of man, every term that comes under the extension of 'man' shares in it. Since Socrates is included in the extension of 'man,' Socrates is said to share in mortality.

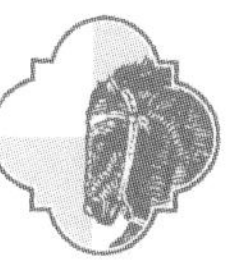

The Dictum de Nullo: ***What is denied universally of a certain term is denied of every term that comes under that term.*** Consider the following argument:

No man is God
Socrates is a man
Therefore, Socrates is not God

This argument denies divinity universally of men. Since 'Socrates' comes under 'men,' it is denied of Socrates too.

Categorical syllogisms state the identity of two terms, the minor term and the major term, by virtue of their mutual identity with a third term, the middle term.

____________ **Summary.** In this chapter, we began discussing the syllogism. We explained that the ***syllogism*** is the verbal expression of a deductive inference. We explained that ***deductive inference*** is one kind of reasoning. We defined ***reasoning*** as "the act by which the mind acquires new knowledge by means of what it already knows." We said that all reasoning assumes the ***Essential Law of Argumentation***, which says, "If the antecedent is true, the consequent must also be true." We defined ***deductive inference*** as "the act by which our mind establishes a connection between the antecedent and the consequent." We defined the ***syllogism*** as "a group of propositions in orderly sequence, one of which (the ***consequent***) is said to be necessarily inferred from the others (the ***antecedent***)."

We said that there are three terms in a syllogism: the major, minor, and middle terms. The ***major term*** is the predicate of the conclusion, the ***minor term*** is the subject of the conclusion, and the ***middle term*** is the term which appears in both premises, but not in the conclusion. We said also that any syllogism contains two premises: a major premise and a minor premise. The ***major premise*** is the premise which contains the major term, and the ***minor premise*** is the premise which contains the minor term.

We said also that in a properly formed syllogism, the major premise is put first and the minor premise second. Finally, we explained the four principles that are fundamental to all logical thought: the ***Principle of Reciprocal Identity***, the ***Principal of Reciprocal Non-Identity***, the ***Dictum de Omni***, and the ***Dictum de Nullo***.

_________ **Exercises for Day 1. Peruse the entire chapter. Then read the introductory section at the very beginning of Chapter 10. Read this section carefully and try to understand it as best you can.**

1. What are we discussing in this chapter?

2. Fill out the following chart showing the three aspects of logic: [Review]

Mental Act	Verbal Expression
■ ____________________	■ ____________________
■ ____________________	■ ____________________
■ ____________________	■ ____________________

Read "Reasoning." Read it carefully.

3. What is the definition of 'reasoning'?

4. What are the two kinds of reasoning?

5. Which of these (the two kinds of reasoning in Question 4) are we studying in this book?

6. Give a brief explanation of the three steps involved in the reasoning process.

7. What are the first two steps together called?

8. What is the last step in the reasoning process called?

9. Why is the conclusion of a syllogism called a conclusion?

10. What is the definition of 'deductive inference'?

11. What is the definition of 'syllogism'?

12. Identify the antecedents and the consequents in the following syllogisms. (Keep in mind that every premise is considered an antecedent and that the consequent is the same as the conclusion.)

    All men are mortal
    Socrates is a man
    Therefore, Socrates is mortal

    No men are gods
    Socrates is a man
    Therefore, Socrates is not a god

    All birds are able to fly
    The ostrich is a bird
    Therefore, the ostrich is able to fly

All apostles are men
Peter is an apostle
Therefore, Peter is a man

All fish can live out of water
A dog is a fish
Therefore, a dog can live out of water

All men are sinners
My dog Spot is a man
Therefore, my dog Spot is a sinner

No ducks are birds
A Mallard is a duck
Therefore, a mallard is not a bird

All reptiles can fly
A horse is a reptile
Therefore, a horse can fly

No beliefs that conflict with the Bible are true
The belief that the world is a product of chance conflicts with the Bible
Therefore, the belief that the world is a product of chance is not true

Read "Validity." Read it carefully.

13. What is the Essential Law of Argumentation?

14. What is the first corollary to the Essential Law of Argumentation?

15. What is the second corollary to the Essential Law of Argumentation?

16. Go back to the arguments listed in Question 12 and write *C1* next to the arguments which are examples of corollary 1 and *C2* next to those that are examples of corollary 2.

Exercises for Day 2. **Read "Terms in a Syllogism." Read it carefully.**

17. What are the three terms contained in a syllogism?

18. Explain how to distinguish each of the following:

    Major term
    Minor term
    Middle term

19. In a syllogism, which premise is the major premise?

20. In a syllogism, which premise is the minor premise?

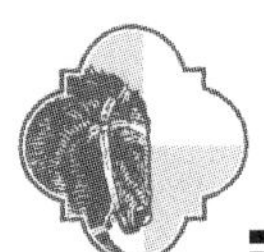

21. In the following syllogisms, indicate which is the major premise and the minor premise by writing *major* or *minor* next to the appropriate premise. Indicate also the minor, major, and middle terms by writing an *S* next to the minor term, a *P* next to the major term, and an *M* next to the middle term.

All men are mortal
Socrates is a man
Therefore, Socrates is mortal

All logic problems are difficult
This problem is a logic problem
Therefore, this problem is difficult

All good basketball players can shoot well
Michael Jordan is a good basketball player
Therefore, Michael Jordan can shoot well

No men are gods
Socrates is a man
Therefore, Socrates is not a god

All apostles are men
Peter is an apostle
Therefore, Peter is a man

No beliefs that conflict with the Bible are true
The belief that the world was created by chance conflicts with the Bible
Therefore, the belief that the world was created by chance is not true

________ Exercises for Day 3. **Read "The Principles of the Syllogism." Read it carefully.**

22. What is the Principle of Reciprocal Identity?

23. What is the Principle of Reciprocal Non-Identity?

24. What is the Dictum de Omni?

25. What is the Dictum de Nullo?

26. Indicate whether the following syllogisms illustrate the Principle of Reciprocal Identity (PRI) or the Principle of Reciprocal Non-Identity (PRNI) and the Dictum de Omni (DO) or the Dictum de Nullo (DN) by circling the appropriate answer. Be aware that a syllogism can illustrate both PRI or PRNI (but not both) <u>and</u> DO or DN (but not both.) In other words, you could circle PRI and DO, but not PRI and PRNI:

All men are mortal
Socrates is a man
Therefore, Socrates is mortal

■ PRI ■ DO
■ PRNI ■ DN

All logic problems are difficult This problem is a logic problem Therefore, this problem is difficult	■ PRI ■ PRNI	■ DO ■ DN
All good basketball players can shoot well Michael Jordan is a good basketball player Therefore, Michael Jordan can shoot well	■ PRI ■ PRNI	■ DO ■ DN
No men are gods Socrates is a man Therefore, Socrates is not a god	■ PRI ■ PRNI	■ DO ■ DN
No beliefs that conflict with the Bible are true The belief that the world was created by chance conflicts with the Bible Therefore, the belief that the world was created by chance is not true	■ PRI ■ PRNI	■ DO ■ DN
All apostles are men Peter is an apostle Therefore, Peter is a man	■ PRI ■ PRNI	■ DO ■ DN

________ Exercises for Day 4.

27. In the following syllogisms, indicate which is the major premise and the minor premise by writing *major* or *minor* next to the appropriate premise. Indicate also the minor, major, and middle terms by writing an *S* next to the minor term, a *P* next to the major term, and an *M* next to the middle term.

    All mammals breathe oxygen
    A horse is a mammal
    Therefore, a horse breathes oxygen

    All Americans are brave
    George Washington is an American
    Therefore, George Washington is brave

    All horses are fast
    Secretariat is a horse
    Therefore, Secretariat is fast

    All wars are bloody
    The War of the Roses was a war
    Therefore, the War of the Roses was bloody

28. Think of five of your own syllogisms that comply with the Essential Rule of Argumentation.

29. Indicate whether the following statements are true or false:

T	F	Reasoning is the act of the mind by which we create new knowledge out of nothing.
T	F	The two kinds of reasoning are deduction and induction.
T	F	A syllogism contains three premises and a conclusion.
T	F	In a valid argument, if the premises are true, the conclusion must be true.
T	F	The minor term is the subject of the conclusion and the major term is the predicate of the conclusion.
T	F	The major premise is the premise that contains the major term.
T	F	The middle term is the term that does not appear in either premise.
T	F	If S is identical with M, and P is identical with M, then S is identical with P.

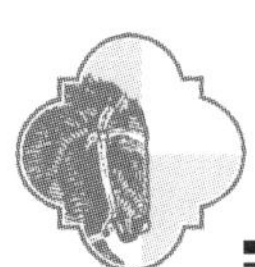

Terminological Rules for Categorical Syllogisms

Introduction. There are seven rules of validity for categorical syllogisms. Remember that a syllogism is said to be valid when the conclusion logically follows from the premises. These seven rules can be broken down into three categories: terminological rules, quantitative rules, and qualitative rules.

Terminological Rules:
I. There must be three and only three terms.
II. The middle term must not occur in the conclusion.

Quantitative Rules:
III. If a term is distributed in the conclusion, then it must be distributed in the premises.
IV. The middle term must be distributed at least once.

Qualitative Rules:
V. No conclusion can follow from two negative premises.
VI. If the two premises are affirmative, the conclusion must also be affirmative.
VII. If either premise is negative, the conclusion must be negative.

There are seven rules governing the validity of categorical syllogisms, which can be listed in three categories: *terminological*, *quantitative*, and *qualitative*.

A syllogism must comply with all of these rules in order for it to be considered valid. If a syllogism violates even one of them, then its conclusion cannot be considered to logically follow from the premises. In this chapter, we will consider the first category of rules, that is, rules I and II. These two rules are considered ***terminological*** because they have specifically to do with the terms in a syllogism.

Rule I: There Must be Three and Only Three Terms. We said in Chapter 10 that every syllogism must have a major term, a minor term, and a middle term. Altogether, then, a syllogism must have three terms. If it has more or less than three terms, then it violates this rule.

This rule can be violated in one of two ways. First, there can be more than three clearly distinguishable terms. If this happens, we are said to have committed the ***Fallacy of Four Terms***. Here is an example of this fallacy:

All mammals have hair
All horses have manes
Therefore, some mammals have hair

If you look at the two statements that are premises in this argument, you can see that we can conclude nothing from them because they contain four terms altogether. None of these terms are connected together in any way. But we can take three of these terms and make a valid argument out of them:

All mammals have hair
All horses are mammals
Therefore, all horses have hair

A syllogism must have three terms. If it has any more or less, then it violates Rule I.

This argument complies with Rule I. It is valid because two of the terms, 'horse' (the minor term) and 'hair' (the major term), are properly connected together by a middle term, 'mammal.' This was not the case with the first argument.

The second (and more common) way this rule can be violated is by the use of an ambiguous middle term. This is called the ***Fallacy of Equivocation***. The Fallacy of Equivocation is harder to spot, since the error it involves is much more subtle.

Remember that in Chapter 3 we said that two terms are equivocal when they are spelled and pronounced exactly alike but have entirely different and unrelated meanings. One example of an equivocal term was 'plane.' The word 'plane' can mean either a flying machine or a geometrical figure (in Geometry, a plane is a flat, even surface, sort of like a piece of paper when it is lying flat). When we use such a term in an argument in both its different meanings, we commit the Fallacy of Equivocation. For example, suppose we make the following argument:

All planes are two-dimensional
All 747s are planes
Therefore, all 747s are two-dimensional

In this syllogism, the middle term, 'plane,' is used equivocally, that is, in two different senses. It is used in the first premise to mean the geometrical figure we call a 'plane.' In the second premise, however, the term is used to mean a flying machine. We have, therefore, committed the Fallacy of Equivocation, since, although the two middle terms look the same, they are not really, and thus we are using more than three terms.

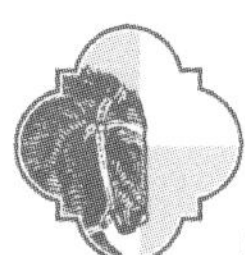

Rule II: The Middle Term Must Not Occur in the Conclusion.

Again, the middle term is the term that connects the two terms that appear in the conclusion: the major term and the minor term. If the middle term appears in the conclusion, then it would have to stand in the place of the minor or major term, meaning that they could not be connected together.

Let's look at the following syllogism:

All plants are living things
All animals are living things
Therefore all living things are plants or animals

Notice that the middle term appears in the conclusion as well as in both premises. This is an example of a syllogism that violates Rule II.

If the middle term appears in the conclusion, then it would have to stand in the place of the minor or major term, meaning that they could not be connected together.

Summary. This chapter concerns the first two of the seven rules with which syllogisms must comply in order to be considered valid. These first two rules are called terminological rules.

Rule I says that there must be three and only three terms in the syllogism. This rule can be violated in two ways. First, it is violated when there are more than three terms in the syllogism. This is called the ***Fallacy of Four Terms***. It is also violated when the middle term is used equivocally. This is called the ***Fallacy of Equivocation***.

Rule II says that the middle term must not occur in the conclusion.

______________ **Exercises for Day 1.** **Peruse the entire chapter. Then read the introductory section at the very beginning of Chapter 11. Read this section carefully and try to understand it as best you can.**

1. What are we discussing in this chapter?

2. Describe each of the seven rules for the validity of a syllogism, indicating the type of rule it is (i.e., terminological, quantitative, or qualitative).

3. How many of these rules does a syllogism have to comply with in order to be considered valid?

4. Which two of these rules do we discuss in this chapter?

5. Why are these rules called 'terminological' rules?

6. What are the three terms contained in a syllogism? [Review]

7. Explain how to distinguish major, minor, and middle terms. [Review]

8. In a syllogism, which premise is the minor premise? [Review]

9. In a syllogism, which premise is the major premise? [Review]

10. In the following syllogisms, indicate which is the major premise and which is the minor premise by writing *major* or *minor* next to the appropriate premise. Indicate also the minor, major, and middle terms by using *S*, *P*, and *M*. [Review]

    All plants are living things
    A daisy is a plant
    Therefore, a daisy is a living thing

    All angels are created by God
    Gabriel is an angel
    Therefore, Gabriel is created by God

    All men are sinners
    I am a man
    Therefore, I am a sinner

    No animal is rational
    My dog Spot is an animal
    Therefore, my dog Spot is not rational

______________ **Exercises for Day 2.** **Read "Rule I: There Must be Three and Only Three Terms." Read it carefully.**

11. What is Rule I?

12. Indicate the two ways in which this rule can be violated.

13. Explain the Fallacy of Four Terms.

14. Explain the Fallacy of Equivocation.

15. What does it mean when a term is equivocal?

16. Indicate whether the following syllogisms are examples of the Fallacy of Four Terms (FFT) or the Fallacy of Equivocation (FE) by circling FFT or FE:

All wildebeasts are mammals
All lions are felines
Therefore, all felines are mammals
■ FFT ■ FE

All animals are irrational
All dogs are mammals
Therefore, all mammals are irrational
■ FFT ■ FE

All accidents are life-threatening
This new recipe was an accident
Therefore, this new recipe is life-threatening
■ FFT ■ FE

All banks contain money
All rivers have banks
Therefore, all rivers contain money
■ FFT ■ FE

All mice eat cheese
Some computer parts are mice
Therefore, some computer parts eat cheese
■ FFT ■ FE

All kings are powerful
No queens are men
Therefore, some men are powerful
■ FFT ■ FE

All aliens are from outer space
All foreigners are aliens
Therefore, foreigners are from outer space
■ FFT ■ FE

All roses have thorns
All flowers are beautiful
Therefore, beautiful things have thorns
■ FFT ■ FE

__________ Exercises for Day 3.

17. Convert the syllogisms you marked FFT (Fallacy of Four Terms) in Question 16 above into syllogisms that comply with Rule I. In other words, use three of the four terms you find in them and construct an argument that has a major term, a minor term, and a middle term.

Read "Rule II: The Middle Term Must Not Occur in the Conclusion." Read it carefully.

18. What is Rule II?

19. Indicate whether the syllogisms below violate Rule II (simply write *Yes* or *No*):

All lions are felines
All felines are animals
Therefore, some felines are lions

All animals are irrational
All horses are animals
Therefore, all horses are irrational

All animals are living beings
All mice are animals
Therefore, all mice are living beings

Some men are kings
All kings are powerful
Therefore, some kings are men

All things life-threatening should be avoided
All accidents are life-threatening
Therefore, all accidents should be avoided

All aliens are supposed to be registered
All foreigners are aliens
Therefore, all foreigners are supposed to be registered

All things that contain water are wet
All rivers contain water
Therefore, all rivers are wet

All flowers are beautiful
All beautiful things should be admired
Therefore, some beautiful things have flowers

20. Circle the middle terms in the syllogisms in Question 19.
(The middle term in these cases will be the term that appears in both premises.)

_________ Exercises for Day 4. Read "Summary." Read it carefully.

21. Using the terms in the syllogisms you found to be invalid in Question 19, construct five syllogisms that comply with Rules I and II.

22. In the following syllogisms, indicate which is the major premise and the minor premise by writing *major* or *minor* in the space provided. Indicate also the minor, major, and middle terms by using *S*, *P*, and *M*. Determine whether the syllogism is valid or invalid. If it is invalid, tell whether it violates Rule I or Rule II. (Hint: if you have a hard time determining the minor and major terms, it is probably because it violates one of these rules.)

A horse is a quadruped
All mammals breathe oxygen
Therefore, some mammals are quadrupeds

All Romans were brave
Julius Caesar was a Roman
Therefore, Julius Caesar was brave

All horses are fast
Secretariat is a horse
Therefore, some horses are fast

All food should be eaten
This logic problem is food for thought
Therefore, this logic problem should be eaten

23. Think of five syllogisms on your own that comply with Rules I and II.

24. Indicate whether the following statements are true or false:

T	F	In order for a syllogism to be valid, it must comply with all seven rules.
T	F	A syllogism must have a minor, major, and middle term.
T	F	If a syllogism commits the Fallacy of Four Terms, that means it does not contain enough terms.
T	F	In a valid syllogism, the minor and major term are connected together by the middle term.
T	F	The Fallacy of Equivocation is easier to spot than the Fallacy of Four Terms.

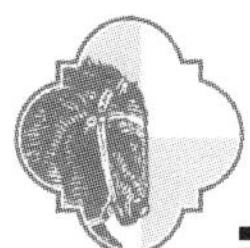

T F Rules I and II are considered terminological rules because they have to do with the nature of the terms in a syllogism.

T F A syllogism violates Rule II when more than one middle term appears in the premises.

T F The minor term is the subject of the conclusion.

Review Exercises for Day 4.

25. What is the definition of 'reasoning'?

26. Give a brief explanation of the three steps involved in the reasoning process.

27. What is the definition of 'syllogism'?

28. What is the Essential Law of Argumentation?

29. What is the first corollary to the Essential Law of Argumentation?

30. What is the second corollary to the Essential Law of Argumentation?

31. What is the Principle of Reciprocal Identity?

32. What is the Principle of Reciprocal Non-Identity?

33. What is the Dictum de Omni?

34. What is the Dictum de Nullo?

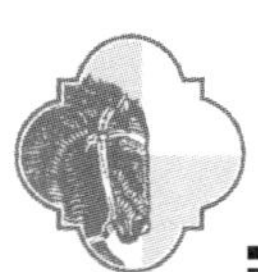

Quantitative Rules for Categorical Syllogisms

Introduction. As we said at the beginning of the last chapter, there are seven rules of validity for categorical syllogisms. In the last chapter we discussed the first two, which we called ***terminological*** rules, since they are concerned with the proper use of terms in a syllogism. In this chapter we will discuss the second group of rules, which we call ***quantitative*** rules.

Let us first review all seven of the rules:

Terminological Rules:
I. There must be three and only three terms.
II. The middle term must not occur in the conclusion.

Quantitative Rules:
III. If a term is distributed in the conclusion, then it must be distributed in the premises.
IV. The middle term must be distributed at least once.

Qualitative Rules:
V. No conclusion can follow from two negative premises.
VI. If the two premises are affirmative, the conclusion must also be affirmative.
VII. If either premise is negative, the conclusion must be negative.

The two rules we will discuss in this chapter are called quantitative rules because they have to do with the quantity of the statements in a syllogism.

As we said, a syllogism must comply with all of these rules in order for it to be considered valid. The two rules we discuss in this chapter are called ***quantitative*** because they have to do with the quantity of the statements in a syllogism. The quantity of a statement, remember, has to do with whether the statement is universal or particular.

Let us begin, then, with Rule III.

__________ **Rule III: If a Term is Distributed in the Conclusion, Then it Must be Distributed in the Premises.** This rule prevents us from trying to say more in the conclusion than is contained in the premises. In order to understand this, we must first recall what it means to say that a term is distributed.

Let us go back to Chapter 8, in which we gave a definition of distribution:

Distribution is the status of a term in regard to its extension.

Extension, remember, has to do with how much a term refers to. When we talked about extension in Part I, we said, for example, that the concept 'man' referred to all possible men; the concept 'animal' referred to all possible animals; etc.

When we say that a term is distributed, we mean that it has full extension. It refers to all possible members of a class. The concept, in other words, *extends* to all the members of a class. When we use the concept 'man,' for example, to refer to all men, we say it is distributed. When we use the concept 'animal,' to refer to all animals, we say that it is ***distributed***. If, on the other hand, a term does not refer to all members of the class it denotes, then we say that it is ***undistributed***.

Rule III prevents us from trying to say more in the conclusion than is contained in the premises.

Take the following syllogism as an example:

All angels are spiritual beings
No men are angels
Therefore, no men are spiritual beings

What the conclusion of the argument assumes is that all spiritual beings are angels; that is the only way the conclusion could logically follow from the premises. But that assumption is nowhere stated in the premises. The conclusion of this argument assumes something that is not in the premises. To say that the terms in the conclusion should both be distributed in the premises is just another way to say this. In other words, the conclusion says more than what the premises say; it goes further than the premises allow. Logically, we can show this by showing that there is a term in the conclusion which is distributed that is not distributed in the premises.

In fact, we know there is something wrong with this syllogism, since we know that men are (at least in part) spiritual beings, and the conclusion denies this, making it false. Yet both the premises are true. How can this be? In fact, we know any syllogism in which the premises are true and the conclusion false is invalid. We know, then, that the syllogism is invalid, but we still have not yet pinpointed why.

How to mark a syllogism: Let us try to show what is wrong with the above syllogism. Let us indicate which terms in the premise are distributed and undistributed by writing a lowercase *d* next to the term when it is distributed and a lowercase *u* if it is undistributed. We will place these letters next to the letter (S, P, or M) that indicates what kind of term it is.

All angels^{Md} are spiritual beings^{Pu}
No men^{Sd} are angels^{Md}
Therefore, no men^{Sd} are spiritual beings^{Pd}

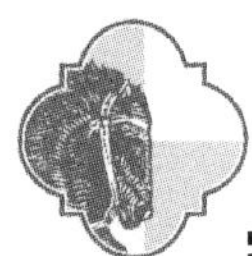

Remember that in Chapter 5 we said there were four basic categorical propositions which take the following form:

A: All S is P
I: Some S is P
E: No S is P
O: Some S is not P

Then in Chapter 8 we said that terms were distributed in different ways in each of these statements. Distribution, we said, has to do with whether a term is used universally or particularly. And we said that in each of these statements, there are two terms: the subject-term and the predicate-term. How did we know which terms were distributed in each of these statements? An easy way to find out would be to look back at the ***Diagram of the Distribution of Terms*** in Chapter 8:

DIAGRAM OF THE DISTRIBUTION OF TERMS IN A, I, E, AND O STATEMENTS

Type of sentence	Subject-Term	Predicate-Term
A	Distributed	Undistributed
I	Undistributed	Undistributed
E	Distributed	Distributed
O	Undistributed	Distributed

We can now look at the syllogism above and determine how terms are distributed in it. The first premise in the syllogism above is an A statement; therefore, while the subject-term ('angels') is distributed, the predicate-term ('spiritual beings') is not. The second premise, on the other hand, is an E statement; therefore, both the subject-term ('men') and the predicate-term ('angels') are distributed. The conclusion, as you see, is an E statement, therefore, again, both the subject-term ('men') and the predicate-term ('spiritual beings') are distributed. If you look at how we have labeled each term, you will see that it complies with the diagram.

In this syllogism, we see that the minor term (S) is distributed (d) in the minor premise (S) and also distributed (d) in the conclusion. Therefore, there is no problem with the minor term. But look at the major term (P). It is undistributed (u) in the first premise, but distributed (d) in the conclusion. This violates Rule III, since there is a term that is distributed in the conclusion that is not distributed in either of the premises. This means that the conclusion is going beyond the premises by stating more than the premises justify. You can't conclude anything about all spiritual beings (which is what the predicate of the conclusion refers to, since it is the predicate of an E statement, and therefore distributed), since the premise only refers to *some* spiritual beings (which is what the predicate of the first premise refers to, since it is the predicate of an A statement and therefore undistributed).

Syllogisms that violate Rule III are said to commit the ***Fallacy of Illicit Process***, and are, as a result, invalid. There are two ways this fallacy is committed. The first is called the Fallacy of Illicit Major. The second is called the Fallacy of Illicit Minor.

There are two ways in which the Fallacy of Illicit Process can be committed: the first is called the *Fallacy of Illicit Major*; the second is called the *Fallacy of Illicit Minor*.

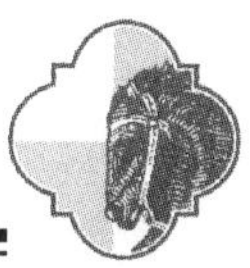

The Fallacy of Illicit Major occurs when the major term (the predicate of the conclusion) is distributed in the conclusion, but not in the major premise. The syllogism we just discussed is an example of the Fallacy of Illicit Major, since the major term, 'spiritual beings,' is distributed in the conclusion, but not in the major premise. It is therefore invalid.

The Fallacy of Illicit Minor occurs when the minor term (the subject of the conclusion) is distributed in the conclusion, but not in the minor premise. An example of the Fallacy of Illicit Minor is as follows:

Rule IV ensures that the major and minor terms get connected in the premises.

All men^{Md} are animals^{Pu}
All men^{Md} are mortal^{Su}
Therefore, all mortals^{Sd} are animals^{Pu}

Here we see that the major term ('animals') is undistributed (u) in both the conclusion and in the major premise. So far, so good. But the minor term ('mortal'), although it is undistributed (u) in the minor premise, is distributed (d) in the conclusion. This violates Rule III. You cannot conclude anything about *all* mortals, because the second premise refers only to *some* mortals. In other words, mortals has greater extension in the conclusion than in the premises, violating Rule III. Since it is the minor term that is distributed in the conclusion but not in the premises, we say it is an example of the Fallacy of Illicit Minor, and therefore invalid.

Rule IV: The Middle Term Must be Distributed at Least Once. Rule IV ensures that the major and minor terms get connected in the premises. Let us look at the following argument:

All angels^{Pd} are spiritual beings^{Mu}
All men^{Sd} are spiritual beings^{Mu}
Therefore, all men^{Sd} are angels^{Pu}

We see that this argument complies with Rule I, since there are three and only three terms; it complies with Rule II, since the middle term does not occur in the conclusion; and it complies with Rule III, since there are no terms distributed in the conclusion that are not distributed in one of the premises. But there is something else wrong with it. Although both premises are true, we know the conclusion to be false. What is wrong?

Since the middle term, 'spiritual beings,' is not distributed in either premise, it cannot serve to connect the minor and major terms, as is necessary in order to come to a conclusion. In other words, as in Rule III, the premises are insufficient to justify the conclusion.

When we violate this rule, we say that we have committed the ***Fallacy of Undistributed Middle***.

Summary. This chapter concerns the second two of the seven rules with which syllogisms must comply in order to be considered valid. These second two rules are called ***quantitative*** rules.

Rule III says that ***if a term is not distributed in the premises, it cannot be distributed in the conclusion***. When we violate this rule we commit the ***Fallacy of Illicit Process***. There are two forms of this fallacy. The first is called the ***Fallacy of Illicit Major***. This fallacy is committed when the term that is distributed in the conclusion but not in the premises is the major term. The second is called the ***Fallacy of Illicit Minor***. This fallacy is committed when the term that is distributed in the conclusion but not in the premises is the minor term.

Rule IV says that ***the middle term must be distributed at least once***. When we violate this rule we are said to have committed the ***Fallacy of Undistributed Middle***.

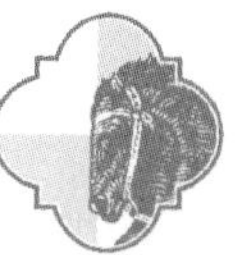

_____________ **Exercises for Day 1. Peruse the entire chapter. Pay particular attention to the summary. Then read the introductory section at the very beginning of Chapter 12. Read this section carefully and try to understand it as best you can.**

1. What are we discussing in this chapter?

2. Write out all seven rules for the validity of categorical syllogisms.

3. How many of these rules does a syllogism have to comply with in order to be considered to be valid?

4. Which two of these rules do we discuss in this chapter?

5. Why are these rules called 'qu6antitative' rules?

6. With what does a statement's quantity have to do?

7. What are the three terms contained in a syllogism? [Review]

8. Explain how to distinguish major, minor, and middle terms. [Review]

9. In a syllogism, which premise is the major premise? [Review]

10. In a syllogism, which premise is the minor premise? [Review]

Read "Rule III: If a Term is Distributed in the Conclusion, Then it Must be Distributed in the Premises."

11. What is Rule III?

12. What does this rule prevent us from trying to do?

13. What is the definition of 'distribution'?

14. With what does extension have to do?

15. When we say that a term is distributed, what do we mean?

16. When we say that a term is undistributed, what do we mean?

17. In marking a syllogism, how do you show that a term is distributed?

18. How do you show that a term is undistributed?

_________ Exercises for Day 2.

19. Fill in the following diagram showing which terms are distributed and which undistributed in different kinds of categorical statements:

DIAGRAM OF THE DISTRIBUTION OF TERMS IN A, I, E, AND O STATEMENTS

Type of sentence	Subject-Term	Predicate-Term	Categorical Statements
A	________	________	____________
I	________	________	____________
E	________	________	____________
O	________	________	____________

20. Mark the following syllogisms, indicating the minor, major, and middle terms (using S, P, and M, respectively) as in the text. Indicate whether the term is distributed or undistributed by writing a lowercase *d* next to the letter that indicates the distributed term(S, P, or M), and a lowercase *u* next to the letter that indicates the undistributed term. (Note that negative statements in which the subject-term is a proper noun are E statements. For example, "Jeff is not rude" is "No S is P," an E statement.)

Example:
All men^{Md} are mortal^{Pu}
Socrates^{Sd} is a man^{Mu}
Therefore, Socrates^{Sd} is mortal^{Pu}

All boys— are human—
Nathaniel— is a boy—
Therefore, Nathaniel— is human—

No boys— are rude—
Jeff— is a boy—
Therefore, Jeff— is not rude—

All cars— are fast—
A Corvette— is a car—
Therefore, a Corvette— is fast—

All girls— are pretty—
Suzy— is a girl—
Therefore, Suzy— is pretty—

All kings— are good—
Hussein— is a king—
Therefore, Hussein— is good—

No truth— is simple—
Christianity— is the truth—
Therefore, Christianity— is not simple—

All Romans— are brave—
Caesar— is a Roman—
Therefore, Caesar— is brave—

All generals— are great—
Hannibal— is a general—
Therefore, Hannibal— is great—

No wars— are fun—
World War II— was a war—
Therefore, World War II— was no fun—

21. Syllogisms that violate Rule III are said to commit what fallacy?

22. In what two ways can this fallacy be committed?

23. Explain the Fallacy of Illicit Major.

24. Explain the Fallacy of Illicit Minor.

25. Circle the Rule that is violated in the following syllogisms. Indicate minor, major, and middle terms (S, P, and M) and whether the terms are distributed or undistributed (d and u) to help determine if Rule III is violated. If Rule III is violated, indicate which fallacy is committed, Illicit Major (IMj) or Illicit Minor (IMn). If no fallacy is committed, then do not mark.

Example:
All boys^{Md} are human^{Pu}
No girls^{Sd} are boys^{Md}
Therefore, no girls^{Sd} are human^{Pd}
■ Rule I ■ Rule II
Rule III: ■ IMn ■ IMj

All victories— are glorious—
No defeat— is a victory—
Therefore, no defeat— is glorious—
■ Rule I ■ Rule II
Rule III: ■ IMn ■ IMj

All men— are animals—
All men— are mortal—
Therefore, all mortals— are animals—
■ Rule I ■ Rule II
Rule III: ■ IMn ■ IMj

No boys— are cowards—
All Latin students— are boys—
Therefore, no Latin students— are cowards—
■ Rule I ■ Rule II
Rule III: ■ IMn ■ IMj

All cars— are fast—
My car— is a Corvette—
Therefore, my car— is fast—
■ Rule I ■ Rule II
Rule III: ■ IMn ■ IMj

All girls— eat cookies—
All Girl Scouts— sell cookies—
Therefore, all girls— are Girl Scouts—
■ Rule I ■ Rule II
Rule III: ■ IMn ■ IMj

All towns— are safe—
Jerusalem— has high walls—
Therefore, Jerusalem— is safe—
■ Rule I ■ Rule II
Rule III: ■ IMn ■ IMj

All Gorgons— have snaky hair—
All Gorgons— are sisters—
Therefore, all sisters— have snaky hair—
■ Rule I ■ Rule II
Rule III: ■ IMn ■ IMj

All Southerners— eat grits—
No Yankee — is a Southerner—
Therefore, no Yankee— eats grits—
■ Rule I ■ Rule II
Rule III: ■ IMn ■ IMj

All Romans— are brave—
No Gaul— is a Roman—
Therefore, no Gaul— is brave—
■ Rule I ■ Rule II
Rule III: ■ IMn ■ IMj

All generals— are great—
All generals— are brave men—
Therefore, all brave men— are great—
■ Rule I ■ Rule II
Rule III: ■ IMn ■ IMj

All wars— are cruel—
No sports games— are wars—
Therefore, no sports games— are cruel—
■ Rule I ■ Rule II
Rule III: ■ IMn ■ IMj

________ **Exercises for Day 3. Read "Rule IV: The Middle Term Must be Distributed at Least Once."**

26. Explain Rule IV.

27. Syllogisms that violate Rule IV are said to commit what fallacy?

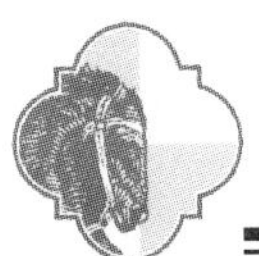

28. Explain the fallacy referred to in Question 27.

29. Indicate which Rule is violated in the following syllogisms. Indicate minor, major, and middle terms (S, P, and M) and whether the terms are distributed or undistributed (d and u) to help determine which rules are violated. If Rule III is violated, indicate which fallacy is committed, Illicit Major (IMj) or Illicit Minor (IMn). If Rule IV is violated, indicate that it has committed the Fallacy of Undistributed Middle (FUM). If no fallacy is committed, then do not mark.

All Gorgons— have snaky hair—
Medusa— has snaky hair—
Therefore, Medusa— is a Gorgon—
■ Rule I ■ Rule II
Rule III: ■ IMn ■ IMj
Rule IV: ■ FUM

No defeat— is glorious—
All victories— are glorious—
Therefore, no victory— is defeat—
■ Rule I ■ Rule II
Rule III: ■ IMn ■ IMj
Rule IV: ■ FUM

All princes— are handsome—
Some toads— are not princes—
Therefore, some toads— are not handsome —
■ Rule I ■ Rule II
Rule III: ■ IMn ■ IMj
Rule IV: ■ FUM

All heroes— are patriots—
Charles Lindbergh— is a hero—
Therefore, Charles Lindbergh— is a patriot—
■ Rule I ■ Rule II
Rule III: ■ IMn ■ IMj
Rule IV: ■ FUM

Some merry men— live in Sherwood Forest—
All archers— are merry men—
Therefore, some archers— live in Sherwood—
■ Rule I ■ Rule II
Rule III: ■ IMn ■ IMj
Rule IV: ■ FUM

All merry men— are archers—
Robin Hood— is an archer—
Therefore, Robin Hood— is a merry man—
■ Rule I ■ Rule II
Rule III: ■ IMn ■ IMj
Rule IV: ■ FUM

All towns— are safe—
Jerusalem— is a town—
Therefore, Jerusalem— is safe—
■ Rule I ■ Rule II
Rule III: ■ IMn ■ IMj
Rule IV: ■ FUM

All queens— are good—
All kings— are good—
Therefore, all kings— are queens—
■ Rule I ■ Rule II
Rule III: ■ IMn ■ IMj
Rule IV: ■ FUM

All opera stars— sing songs—
No sirens— are opera stars—
Therefore, no sirens— sing songs—
■ Rule I ■ Rule II
Rule III: ■ IMn ■ IMj
Rule IV: ■ FUM

Some dull things— are valuable—
All homework— is dull—
Therefore, some homework— is valuable—
■ Rule I ■ Rule II
Rule III: ■ IMn ■ IMj
Rule IV: ■ FUM

Some great generals— defeated Rome—
Hannibal— was a great general—
Therefore, Hannibal— defeated Rome—
■ Rule I ■ Rule II
Rule III: ■ IMn ■ IMj
Rule IV: ■ FUM

All toads— are ugly—
No princes— are toads—
Therefore, no princes— are ugly—
■ Rule I ■ Rule II
Rule III: ■ IMn ■ IMj
Rule IV: ■ FUM

Exercises for Day 4. **Read "Summary." Read it carefully.**

30. Indicate which Rule is violated in the following syllogisms. Indicate minor, major, and middle terms (S, P, and M) and whether the terms are distributed or undistributed (d and u) to help determine which rules are violated. If Rule III is violated, indicate which fallacy is committed, Illicit Major (IMj) or Illicit Minor (IMn). If Rule IV is violated, indicate that it has committed the Fallacy of Undistributed Middle (FUM). If no fallacy is committed, then do not mark.

Some green men— are leprechauns—
Some green men— are Martians—
Therefore, some Martians— are leprechauns—
■ Rule I ■ Rule II
Rule III: ■ IMn ■ IMj
Rule IV: ■ FUM

All leopards— are felines—
All lions— are felines—
Therefore, some lions— are leopards—
■ Rule I ■ Rule II
Rule III: ■ IMn ■ IMj
Rule IV: ■ FUM

All oaks— are trees—
No maples— are oaks—
Therefore, no maples— are trees—
■ Rule I ■ Rule II
Rule III: ■ IMn ■ IMj
Rule IV: ■ FUM

No irrational thing— is a man—
All beasts— are irrational—
Therefore, no beast— is a man—
■ Rule I ■ Rule II
Rule III: ■ IMn ■ IMj
Rule IV: ■ FUM

All towns— are safe—
Jerusalem— is a holy city—
Therefore, some holy cities— are safe—
■ Rule I ■ Rule II
Rule III: ■ IMn ■ IMj
Rule IV: ■ FUM

Some rodents— are a threat—
All mice— are rodents—
Therefore, no mice— are a threat—
■ Rule I ■ Rule II
Rule III: ■ IMn ■ IMj
Rule IV: ■ FUM

All kings— are good—
All kings— are rich—
Therefore, all rich people— are good—
■ Rule I ■ Rule II
Rule III: ■ IMn ■ IMj
Rule IV: ■ FUM

All ducks— are birds —
All birds— have feathers—
Therefore, some birds— are not ducks —
■ Rule I ■ Rule II
Rule III: ■ IMn ■ IMj
Rule IV: ■ FUM

31. Think of five of your own syllogisms that comply with Rules I, II, III, and IV. (Try to use a mix of A, E, I, and O statements.)

32. Indicate whether the following statements are true or false:

T	F	If a term is distributed in the conclusion, it must be distributed in the premises.
T	F	The subject-term of an E statement is distributed.
T	F	Syllogisms that violate Rule IV are said to commit the Fallacy of Illicit Process.
T	F	The Fallacy of Illicit Major is committed when the major term is distributed in the conclusion, but not in the premises.
T	F	If the middle term is not distributed in either of the premises, then the syllogism is invalid.
T	F	The Fallacy of Undistributed Middle is committed when the middle term is distributed in the premises but not in the conclusion.

Qualitative Rules for Categorical Syllogisms

Introduction. We now turn to the qualitative rules for categorical syllogisms. In the last chapter, we discussed quantitative rules and in the chapter before that, terminological rules. Just as terminological rules have to do with how terms are arrayed in a syllogism and quantitative rules have to do with the quantity of the statements in the syllogism, qualitative rules have to do with the quality of the statements in the syllogism.

Let us once again review all seven of the rules:

Terminological Rules:
I. There must be three and only three terms.
II. The middle term must not occur in the conclusion.

Quantitative Rules:
III. If a term is distributed in the conclusion, then it must be distributed in the premises.
IV. The middle term must be distributed at least once.

Qualitative Rules:
V. No conclusion can follow from two negative premises.
VI. If the two premises are affirmative, the conclusion must also be affirmative.
VII. If either premise is negative, the conclusion must be negative.

Once again, a syllogism must comply with all of these rules in order for it to be considered valid. The three rules we discuss in this chapter are called ***qualitative*** because they have to do with the quality of the statements in a syllogism. The quality of a statement, remember, has to do with whether it is affirmative or negative.

The three rules we will discuss in this chapter are called qualitative rules because they have to do with the quality of the statements in a syllogism.

__________ Rule V: No Conclusion Can Follow from Two Negative Premises. This rule prevents us, as several other rules do, from trying to say more in the conclusion than is contained in the premises. When we have two negative premises, we cannot establish a connection between the major and minor term.

Let's look at an example of a syllogism that violates Rule V:

No plants are animals
Some minerals are not animals
Therefore, some minerals are not plants

Here you can see that both premises are true, as well as the conclusion. But does the conclusion follow from the premises? No, it does not. From the fact that no plants are animals and the fact that some minerals are not animals, it does not logically follow that some minerals are not plants. The reason, in this case, that the argument is invalid is that both of its premises are negative.

This syllogism complies with all the other rules, but it does not comply with Rule V. When this rule is broken, we say it commits the ***Fallacy of Exclusive Premises***.

No matter how hard we try, we cannot logically derive a negative conclusion from two affirmative premises.

__________ Rule VI: If the Two Premises are Affirmative, the Conclusion Must Also be Affirmative. No matter how hard we try, we cannot logically derive a negative conclusion from two affirmative premises. An example of how this rule can be violated is as follows:

All men are mortals
All mortals make mistakes
Therefore, some things that make mistakes are not men

Again, this argument complies with all other six rules. But although the conclusion in this syllogism is true, it goes beyond what the premises justify. There may be some other premises that justify it, but not these two.

A syllogism that violates this rule is said to commit the ***Fallacy of Drawing a Negative Conclusion from Affirmative Premises***.

__________ Rule VII: If Either Premise is Negative, the Conclusion Must Also be Negative. An example of a violation of Rule VII would be as follows:

All cannibals are bloodthirsty
Some accountants are not bloodthirsty
Therefore, some accountants are cannibals

Again, this syllogism complies with all the other rules. This says that some accountants are not bloodthirsty. But the conclusion assumes that *only* some accountants are not bloodthirsty. But if all accountants are not bloodthirsty (which is perfectly consistent with saying that some of them are), then the argument falls apart. Just because we say that some are excluded from a group, it does not preclude the possibility that all may be.

Syllogisms that break this rule are said to commit the ***Fallacy of Drawing an Affirmative Conclusion from a Negative Premise***.

____________ **Summary.** This chapter concerns the last set of the seven rules with which syllogisms must comply in order to be considered valid. The rules in this last set are called ***qualitative*** rules.

Rule V says that ***no conclusion can follow from two negative premises***. When we violate this rule we commit the ***Fallacy of Exclusive Premises***.

Rule VI says that ***if the two premises are affirmative, the conclusion must also be affirmative***. When we violate this rule we say we commit the ***Fallacy of Drawing a Negative Conclusion from Affirmative Premises***.

Rule VII says that ***if either premise is negative, the conclusion must also be negative***. When we violate this rule we are said to have committed the ***Fallacy of Drawing an Affirmative Conclusion from a Negative Premise***.

_____ **Exercises for Day 1. Peruse the entire chapter. Read the introductory section at the very beginning of Chapter 13. Read this section carefully and try to understand it as best you can.**

1. What are we discussing in this chapter?

2. Describe each of the seven rules for the validity of syllogisms. [Review]

3. How many of these rules does a syllogism have to comply with in order to be considered valid? [Review]

4. Which three of these rules do we discuss in this chapter?

5. Why are these rules called 'qualitative' rules?

6. With what does a statement's quality have to do?

7. What are the three terms contained in a syllogism? [Chapter 10 Review]

8. Explain how to distinguish the major, minor, and middle terms. [Chapter 10 Review]

9. In a syllogism, which premise is the minor premise? [Chapter 10 Review]

10. In a syllogism, which premise is the major premise? [Chapter 10 Review]

11. Fill in the following diagram, showing which terms are distributed and which are undistributed in different kinds of categorical statements by writing *distributed* or *undistributed* in the blanks:

DIAGRAM OF THE DISTRIBUTION OF TERMS IN A, I, E, AND O STATEMENTS

Type of sentence	Subject-Term	Predicate-Term	Categorical Statements
A	_____	_____	_____
I	_____	_____	_____
E	_____	_____	_____
O	_____	_____	_____

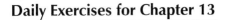

__________ **Exercises for Day 2.** **Read "Rule V: No Conclusion Can Follow from Two Negative Premises."**

12. What is Rule V?

13. What does this rule prevent us from trying to do?

14. Syllogisms that violate Rule V are said to commit what fallacy?

15. Indicate which Rule is violated in the following syllogisms. Indicate minor, major, and middle terms (S, P, and M) and whether the terms are distributed or undistributed (d and u) to help determine if Rule V is violated. If no fallacy is committed, then do not mark.

No saints— are villains—
Some robbers— are not villains———
Therefore, some robbers— are saints—
■ Rule I ■ Rule II
■ Rule III ■ Rule IV ■ Rule V

All floods— are devastating—
No drought— is a flood—
Therefore, no drought— is devastating—
■ Rule I ■ Rule II
■ Rule III ■ Rule IV ■ Rule V

All Protestants— believe in the Trinity—
All Catholics— believe in the Trinity—
Therefore, some Catholics— are Protestant—
■ Rule I ■ Rule II
■ Rule III ■ Rule IV ■ Rule V

No Greeks— are Romans—
Some soldiers— are not Romans—
Therefore, some soldiers— are not Greeks—
■ Rule I ■ Rule II
■ Rule III ■ Rule IV ■ Rule V

No tornadoes—are pleasant—
Some violent storms— are tornadoes—
Therefore, no violent storms— are pleasant—
■ Rule I ■ Rule II
■ Rule III ■ Rule IV ■ Rule V

Some vegetables— are not sweet—
No vegetable— is a fruit—
Therefore, some fruits— are not sweet—
■ Rule I ■ Rule II
■ Rule III ■ Rule IV ■ Rule V

All symphonies— are beautiful—
No opera— is a symphony—
Therefore, no opera— is beautiful—
■ Rule I ■ Rule II
■ Rule III ■ Rule IV ■ Rule V

No maples— are pines —
No oaks— are pines—
Therefore, no oaks— are maples—
■ Rule I ■ Rule II
■ Rule III ■ Rule IV ■ Rule V

No man— is as wise as Solomon—
Einstein— is a man—
Therefore, Einstein— is not as wise as Solomon—
■ Rule I ■ Rule II
■ Rule III ■ Rule IV ■ Rule V

Some merry men—are not in Sherwood Forest—
No sheriff— is a merry man—
Therefore, no sheriff— is in Sherwood Forest—
■ Rule I ■ Rule II
■ Rule III ■ Rule IV ■ Rule V

_______________ **Exercises for Day 3.** **Read "Rule VI: If the Two Premises are Affirmative the Conclusion Must Also be Affirmative."**

16. Explain Rule VI.

17. Syllogisms that violate Rule VI are said to commit what fallacy?

18. Indicate which of the six rules is violated in the following syllogisms. Indicate minor, major, and middle terms (S, P, and M) and whether the terms are distributed or undistributed (d and u) to help determine which rules are violated. If no fallacy is committed, then do not mark.

All mermaids— can swim—
Some nymphs— are mermaids—
Therefore, some nymphs— are not swimmers—
■ Rule I ■ Rule II
■ Rule III ■ Rule IV ■ Rule V
■ Rule VI

All revolutions— are bloody—
No election— is bloody—
Therefore, no election— is a revolution—
■ Rule I ■ Rule II
■ Rule III ■ Rule IV ■ Rule V
■ Rule VI

All archers— are foresters—
All foresters— are merry men—
Therefore, some merry men—aren't archers—
Rule I ■ Rule II
■ Rule III ■ Rule IV ■ Rule V
■ Rule VI

No boys— are rude—
No girls— are boys—
Therefore, no girls— are rude—
■ Rule I ■ Rule II
■ Rule III ■ Rule IV ■ Rule V
■ Rule VI

All queens— are regal—
Elizabeth— is a queen—
Therefore, Elizabeth— is regal—
■ Rule I ■ Rule II
■ Rule III ■ Rule IV ■ Rule V
■ Rule VI

All oaks— are trees —
All trees— are alive—
Therefore, some living things— are not oaks—
■ Rule I ■ Rule II
■ Rule III ■ Rule IV ■ Rule V
■ Rule VI

All teeth— are white—
A molar— is a tooth—
Therefore, a molar— is white—
■ Rule I ■ Rule II
■ Rule III ■ Rule IV ■ Rule V
■ Rule VI

All jesters— are clowns—
All clowns— are funny—
Therefore, some funny people— are not jesters—
■ Rule I ■ Rule II
■ Rule III ■ Rule IV ■ Rule V
■ Rule VI

All military leaders— are male—
Joan of Arc— is not a male—
Therefore, Joan of Arc—is not a military leader—
■ Rule I ■ Rule II
■ Rule III ■ Rule IV ■ Rule V
■ Rule VI

All Romans— are brave—
Some Gauls— are not Romans—
Therefore, some Gauls— are not brave—
■ Rule I ■ Rule II
■ Rule III ■ Rule IV ■ Rule V
■ Rule VI

All moons— are spherical—
All moons— revolve—
Therefore, all things that revolve— are spherical—
■ Rule I ■ Rule II
■ Rule III ■ Rule IV ■ Rule V
■ Rule VI

All beagles— are dogs—
All dogs— are loyal—
Therefore, some loyal things— aren't beagles—
■ Rule I ■ Rule II
■ Rule III ■ Rule IV ■ Rule V
■ Rule VI

_______ Exercises for Day 4. Read "Rule VII: If Either Premise is Negative, the Conclusion Must Also be Negative."

19. Indicate which Rule is violated in the following syllogisms. Indicate minor, major, and middle terms (S, P, and M) and whether the terms are distributed or undistributed (d and u) to help determine which rules are violated. If no fallacy is committed, then do not mark.

Some fairies— are not leprechauns—
All leprechauns— are green men—
Therefore, some green men— are fairies—
■ Rule I ■ Rule II
■ Rule III ■ Rule IV ■ Rule V
■ Rule VI ■ Rule VII

No revolutions— are bloody—
All elections— are bloody—
Therefore, no election— is a revolution—
■ Rule I ■ Rule II
■ Rule III ■ Rule IV ■ Rule V
■ Rule VI ■ Rule VII

No noble thing— is revered—
All heroes— are revered—
Therefore, no hero— is a noble thing—
■ Rule I ■ Rule II
■ Rule III ■ Rule IV ■ Rule V
■ Rule VI ■ Rule VII

All teeth— are white—
All teeth— are molars—
Therefore, some molars— are white—
■ Rule I ■ Rule II
■ Rule III ■ Rule IV ■ Rule V
■ Rule VI ■ Rule VII

No oaks— are pines—
Some trees— are oaks—
Therefore, some trees— are pines—
■ Rule I ■ Rule II
■ Rule III ■ Rule IV ■ Rule V
■ Rule VI ■ Rule VII

No hawks— are warblers—
Some birds— are hawks—
Therefore, some birds— are warblers—
■ Rule I ■ Rule II
■ Rule III ■ Rule IV ■ Rule V
■ Rule VI ■ Rule VII

20. Think of five of your own syllogisms that comply with all seven rules.
(Use as many of the four kinds of categorical statements as you can.)

Read "Summary."

21. Indicate whether the following statements are true or false:

T	F	If there are more than three terms in a syllogism, the syllogism violates Rule III.
T	F	If a syllogism has at least one affirmative premise, the conclusion must be affirmative.
T	F	The Fallacy of Illicit Minor occurs when the minor term is distributed in the conclusion but not in the premises.
T	F	The middle term must be distributed at least once.
T	F	No conclusion can follow from two negative premises.
T	F	The minor term must be universal in both the conclusion and the premises.

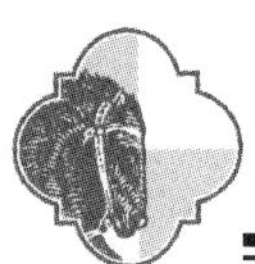

Review

Introduction. In this chapter we will review some of the important aspects of the subject of logic that we have covered since the beginning of the book.

In the introduction to this book, we started out by defining logic as "the science of right thinking." We said there are two main branches of logic. One is called ***formal***, or ***minor***, logic, the other ***material***, or ***major***, logic. Material logic is concerned with the ***content*** of argumentation. Formal logic is interested in the ***form*** or structure of reasoning. We defined ***truth*** as the correspondence with reality, which is of concern in formal logic only as it relates to determining validity. We said an argument is ***valid*** when its conclusion follows logically from its premises. And we said that ***soundness*** indicates that all the premises in an argument are true *and* that the argument is valid.

We said also that all arguments must contain two premises and a conclusion. And we said, finally, that there are three mental acts that make up the logical process: ***simple apprehension***, ***judgment***, and ***deductive inference***. These three mental acts correspond to three verbal expressions: ***term***, ***proposition***, and ***syllogism***.

In fact, let's look again at the chart we concluded with in the introduction of this book:

Mental Act	Verbal Expression
Simple Apprehension	Term
Judgment	Proposition
Deductive Inference	Syllogism

In this chapter we will review some of the important aspects of the subject of logic that we have covered since the beginning of the book.

Simple Apprehension. In Chapter 1 we discussed the meaning of simple apprehension. We said three things generally occur during simple apprehension: we perceive it with our senses, we have a mental image of it, and we conceive the meaning of it. We also said that simple apprehension is an act by which the mind grasps the concept or general meaning of an object without affirming or denying anything about it. We said, finally, that the

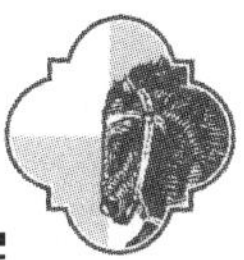

process by which a simple apprehension is derived from a sense perception and a mental image is called ***abstraction***.

_________ **Comprehension and Extension.** In Chapter 2 we discussed the ***properties*** of simple apprehension. We said there are two properties of simple apprehension: ***comprehension*** and ***extension***. The comprehension of a simple apprehension is a description of what a concept is. The extension of a concept is a description of the things to which a concept applies. We said, finally, that the greater the comprehension of a concept, the less its extension; and the greater its extension, the less its comprehension.

The first three chapters dealt with terms. *Term*, remember, is the first of the three aspects of logic.

_________ **Signification and Supposition.** ***Signification*** and ***supposition*** are the two properties of the ***term***, the term being the verbal expression of a simple apprehension. Terms ***signify*** concepts in three different ways: ***univocal*** terms are terms that have exactly the same meaning no matter when or how they are used; ***equivocal*** terms, on the other hand, are terms that, although spelled and pronounced exactly alike, have entirely different and unrelated meanings; ***analogous*** terms, finally, are terms that are applied to different things, but have related meanings.

Just as there are three ways that terms are divided up according to their signification, there are three ways they are divided up according to their supposition. ***Material supposition*** occurs when a term refers to something as it exists verbally; ***logical supposition*** occurs when a term refers to something as it exists logically; and ***real supposition*** occurs when a term refers to something as it exists in the real world.

The first three chapters (not including the Introduction) dealt with terms. ***Term***, remember, is the first of the three aspects of logic. The three aspects of logic are simple apprehension, judgment, and deductive inference. Remember also that these three aspects of logic are verbally expressed by terms, propositions, and syllogisms.

In Chapter 1 we dealt with the definition of simple apprehension. In Chapter 2 we dealt with the properties of simple apprehension. In Chapter 3 we dealt with the properties of term.

We said that a term is a word or group of words which stand for a concept which is applicable to real things. The term 'man,' for example, is a word (which has three letters) which stands for a concept (which by comprehension has five notes and by extension refers to all the men who are, ever were, and ever will be) which refers to real men in the world.

In the chapters that follow, we left the subject of terms and began to discuss how terms relate to one another in propositions (or statements).

_________ **What is Judgment?** In Chapter 4 we moved from the study of term to the study of judgment. We said that ***judgment*** is a mental act whose verbal expression is what we call a proposition. We said that judgment can be defined as the act by which the intellect unites by affirming, or separates by denying. A ***proposition*** is a sentence or statement which expresses truth or falsity. The three elements of any proposition are the ***subject-term***, the ***predicate-term***, and the ***copula***. Finally, sentences are much more easily

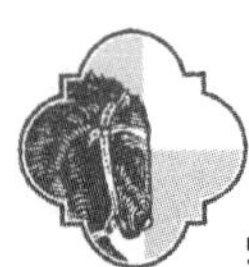

handled in logic if they are put into proper ***logical form***, which means that they must show all three elements of a logical proposition clearly.

_____________ The Four Basic Categorical Propositions. There are four basic categorical propositions with which formal logic deals: "All S is P"; "Some S is P"; "No S is P"; and "Some S is not P." In addition to the three components, the subject-term (S), the predicate-term (P), and the copula (c), there is a fourth component: the quantifier. The quantifiers are the words 'All,' 'Some,' 'No,' and 'Some ... not.'

There are two fundamental characteristics of categorical propositions: quality and quantity. ***Quality*** has to do with whether a statement is ***affirmative*** or ***negative***. ***Quantity*** has to do with whether a proposition is ***universal*** or ***particular***.

A and I statements are affirmative, while E and O statements are negative; this is their quality. A and E statements are universal, while I and O statements are particular; this is their quantity.

We can summarize the quality and quantity of each statement as follows:

Quantity and Quality of the Four Categorical Statements:

		Quality	
		Affirmative	Negative
Quantity	Universal	A	E
	Particular	I	O

_____________ Contradictory and Contrary Statements. In Chapters 6 and 7 we learned that statements can have four different relationships of opposition. According to the ***Rule of Contradiction***, two statements are contradictory if they differ in both quality and quantity. In addition, according to the ***First Law of Opposition***, two contradictory statements cannot both be true at the same time, nor can they both be false at the same time.

The Rule of Contradiction is the test you apply to determine whether two statements are contradictory. If you ever get confused about which statements are contradictory, all you have to do is remember that they must differ in both quality and quantity—and that they are diagonal to each other on the chart (Figure 6-2).

We learned also that, according to the ***Rule of Contraries***, two statements are contrary if they are both universal but differ in quality. Second, according to the ***Second Law of Opposition***, two contraries cannot both be true at the same time, but can, at the same time, both be false.

Again, if you ever get confused about which statements are contrary, all you have to do is remember that they must both be universal but differ in quality—and that they are indicated on the chart (Figure 6-2).

In Chapter 4 we moved from the study of *term* to the study of judgment. We said that *judgment* is a mental act whose verbal expression is what we call a *proposition*.

In Chapters 6-9, we discussed the four basic categorical propositions, the different ways they can be in opposition, and the different ways they can be equivalent.

__________ **Subcontrary and Subalternate Statements.** According to the ***Rule of Subcontraries***, two statements are subcontrary if they are both particular statements that differ in quality. According to the ***Third Law of Opposition***, two subcontraries may at the same time be true, but cannot at the same time be false.

We learned that, according to the ***Rule of Subalterns***, two statements are subalternate if they have the same quality, but differ in quantity. According to the ***Fourth Law of Opposition***, subalterns may both be true or both be false. If the particular is false, the universal is false; if the universal is true, then the particular is true; otherwise their status is indeterminate.

If you ever get confused about which statements are contradictory, contrary, subcontrary, or subalternate, you can consult Figure 7-2, where all the relationships are visually illustrated.

__________ **Distribution.** In Chapter 8 we discussed distribution. ***Distribution*** is the status of a term in regard to its extension. When we say that a term is distributed, we mean that the term refers to all the members of the class of things denoted by the term. We said that the subject-term is distributed in statements whose quantity is universal and undistributed in statements whose quantity is particular. In regard to the predicate-term, we said that in affirmative propositions the predicate-term is always taken particularly (and therefore undistributed), and in negative propositions the predicate is always taken universally (and therefore distributed).

We showed how distribution works with both subject and predicate terms by using the following diagram:

DIAGRAM OF THE DISTRIBUTION OF TERMS IN A, E, I, AND O STATEMENTS

Type of sentence	Subject-Term	Predicate-Term
A	Distributed	Undistributed
I	Undistributed	Undistributed
E	Distributed	Distributed
O	Undistributed	Distributed

Finally, we showed how to use Euler's diagrams to display the distribution of various categorical statements.

__________ **Obversion, Conversion, and Contraposition.** In Chapter 9 we discussed relationships of ***equivalence***. There are three ways statements can be converted into their logical equivalents: obversion, conversion, and contraposition.

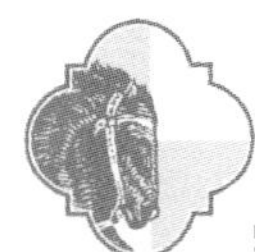

An A statement can be obverted by 1) changing its quality and 2) negating the predicate. ***Obversion*** is permissible with all four kinds of statements. Statements can be obverted in the following way:

All S is P -----------------> No S is not P
No S is P -----------------> All S is not P
Some S is P -------------> Some S is not non-P
Some S is not P ---------> Some S is not P

A statement can be converted by simply interchanging the subject and predicate. ***Conversion*** works only for E and I statements, although true A statements can be partially converted into true I statements. Statements can be converted in the following way:

No S is P --------------------> No P is S
Some S is P -----------------> Some P is S

The syllogism is the verbal expression of deductive inference.

Contraposition is accomplished by first obverting the statement, then converting, and then obverting the statement again. Contraposition may be used only with A and O statements. Statements can be contraposed in the following way:

All S is P ------------------> All non-P is non-S
Some S is not P ---------> Some non-P is S

In Chapters 6-9 we discussed propositions. We discussed the four basic categorical propositions, the different ways they can be in opposition, and the different ways they can be equivalent. Beginning in Chapter 10, we moved from propositions to the study of syllogisms.

____________ **What is Deductive Inference?** In Chapter 10 we explained that the ***syllogism*** is the verbal expression of a deductive inference. ***Deductive inference*** is one kind of reasoning. We defined ***reasoning*** as "the act by which the mind acquires new knowledge by means of what it already knows." All reasoning, we said, assumes the ***Essential Law of Argumentation***, which says, "If the antecedent is true, the consequent must also be true." We defined ***deductive inference*** as "the act by which the mind establishes a connection between the antecedent and the consequent." We defined the ***syllogism*** as "a group of propositions in orderly sequence, one of which (the ***consequent***) is said to be necessarily inferred from the others (the ***antecedent***)."

There are three terms in a syllogism: the major, minor, and middle terms. The ***major term*** is the predicate of the conclusion, the ***minor term*** is the subject of the conclusion, and the ***middle term*** is the term which appears in both premises, but not in the conclusion. We said also that any syllogism contains two premises: a major premise and a minor premise. The ***major premise*** is the premise which contains the major term, and the ***minor premise*** is the premise which contains the minor term.

We said also that in a properly formed syllogism, the major premise is put first and the minor premise second. Finally, we explained the four principles that are fundamental to all logical thought: the ***Principle of Reciprocal Identity***, the ***Principal of Reciprocal Non-Identity***, the ***Dictum de Omni***, and the ***Dictum de Nullo***.

__________ **Terminological Rules for Syllogisms.** Chapter 11 concerns the first two of the seven rules with which syllogisms must comply in order to be considered valid. These first two rules are called ***terminological*** rules.

Rule I says that ***there must be three and only three terms in the syllogism***. This rule can be violated in two ways. First it is violated when there are more than three terms in the syllogism. This is called the ***Fallacy of Four Terms***. It is also violated when the middle term is used equivocally. This is called the ***Fallacy of Equivocation.***

Rule II says that ***the middle term must not occur in the conclusion.***

__________ **Quantitative Rules for Syllogisms.** In Chapter 12 we dealt with the second two of the seven rules with which syllogisms must comply in order to be considered valid. These second two rules are called ***quantitative*** rules because they have to do with the quantity of statements in the syllogism.

Rule III says that ***if a term is not distributed in the premises, it cannot be distributed in the conclusion***. When we violate this rule we commit the ***Fallacy of Illicit Process***. There are two forms of this fallacy. The first is called the ***Fallacy of Illicit Major***. This fallacy is committed when the term that is distributed in the conclusion but not in the premises is the major term. The second is called the ***Fallacy of Illicit Minor***. This fallacy is committed when the term that is distributed in the conclusion but not in the premises is the minor term.

Rule IV says that ***the middle term must be distributed at least once***. When we violate this rule we are said to have committed the ***Fallacy of Undistributed Middle***.

__________ **Qualitative Rules for Syllogisms.** Chapter 13 concerns the last set of the seven rules with which syllogisms must comply in order to be considered valid. These last rules are called ***qualitative*** rules.

Rule V says that ***no conclusion can follow from two negative premises***. When we violate this rule we commit the ***Fallacy of Exclusive Premises***.

Rule VI says that ***if the two premises are affirmative, the conclusion must also be affirmative***. When we violate this rule we say we commit the ***Fallacy of Drawing a Negative Conclusion from Affirmative Premises***.

Rule VII says that ***if either premise is negative, the conclusion must also be negative***. When we violate this rule we are said to have committed the ***Fallacy of Drawing an Affirmative Conclusion from a Negative Premise***.

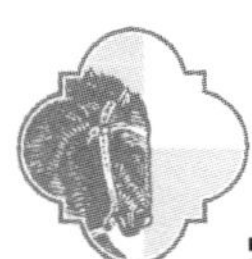

__________ **Summary.** In this book, we have discussed elements of the three aspects of logic: simple apprehension, judgment, and deductive inference. But in many ways we have only scratched the surface. In the second book in this series of logic books, we will discover that syllogisms have certain forms, and by these forms alone, we can determine whether they are valid or not. We will discover that out of the 64 different forms a syllogism can take, only 19 are valid, and only five of these are commonly used. We will discover an easy way to remember them and apply the concepts we learn to arguments that have been made by great thinkers over time.

__________ **Exercises for Day 1. Peruse the entire chapter. Then carefully read "Introduction." Review introductory chapter to this book if necessary.**

1. Write out the chart below listing the mental acts and their corresponding verbal expressions in the order in which we have covered them:

Mental Act	Verbal Expression
■ __________	■ __________
■ __________	■ __________
■ __________	■ __________

Carefully read "Simple Apprehension." Review Chapter 1 if necessary.

2. Indicate whether the following statements are true or false:

T	F	Mental image is the simple apprehension itself.
T	F	A sense perception of something we see disappears when we are no longer looking at it.
T	F	A sense perception of a chair is different from the chair itself because the chair exists in the mind, while the sense perception exists outside the mind.
T	F	Sense perception is the act of seeing or hearing or smelling or tasting or touching.
T	F	When we see something, an image forms in our minds, which we call a mental image.
T	F	A sense perception lasts only as long as we are perceiving the chair through our senses.
T	F	A mental image is the image of an object formed in our minds as a result of a sense perception of that object.
T	F	The idea of a chair in your mind must be accompanied by the sense perception of a chair or by the mental image of a chair.
T	F	Simple apprehension is an act by which the mind grasps the concept or gen eral meaning of an object and affirms or denies something about it.
T	F	The terms 'concept' and 'simple apprehension' mean the same thing.
T	F	A simple apprehension has shape and color.
T	F	When we have a simple apprehension of a thing, we grasp the thing's essence.
T	F	If you have a different mental image of a concept than another person has, then you both cannot be thinking of the same concept.
T	F	The process by which a simple apprehension is derived from a sense perception and mental image is called abstraction.
T	F	If we were to affirm or deny something about a concept, we would be going beyond simple apprehension to judgment.

Carefully read "Comprehension and Extension." Review Chapter 2 if necessary.

3. Indicate whether the following statements are true or false:

T	F	The two properties of simple apprehension are concept and extension.
T	F	The concept 'man' is complex.
T	F	Porphyry once said that a man is a featherless biped.
T	F	If something is sentient, that means that it is something rather than nothing.
T	F	The concept 'man' has four notes.
T	F	The concept 'animal' has greater extension than the concept 'man.'

T F The concept 'man' has greater extension than the concept 'body.'
T F The concept 'man' has greater comprehension than the concept 'body.'
T F The concept 'man' has greater comprehension than the concept 'animal.'

______ Exercises for Day 2. Carefully read "Signification and Supposition." Review Chapter 3 if necessary.

4. Indicate whether the following statements are true or false:

T F Comprehension and extension are two properties of terms.
T F The three ways terms can be divided according to their signification are univocal, equivocal, and analogous.
T F The term 'photosynthesis' is an example of an equivocal term.
T F Univocal terms always mean the same thing.
T F Equivocal terms have related meanings.
T F Analogous terms have entirely different and unrelated meanings.
T F The term 'jar' is an example of an equivocal term.
T F The term 'window' is an example of an equivocal term.
T F Equivocal terms are used in puns.
T F Many analogous terms are scientific terms.
T F The three ways to divide up terms according to their signification is into verbal, mental, and real existence.
T F Material supposition occurs when a term refers to something that exists in the real world.
T F When a term refers to real existence, it is said to be an instance of material supposition.
T F When a term refers to mental existences, it is said to be an instance of logical supposition.
T F The sentence "Man was created by God" is an example of real supposition.
T F The three aspects of logic are simple apprehension, judgment, and deductive inference.

Carefully read "What is Judgment?" Review Chapter 4 if necessary.

5. Indicate whether the following statements are true or false:

T F A proposition is the verbal expression of a judgment.
T F A judgment unites two concepts.
T F Judgment is the third part of the study of logic.
T F The subject and the copula are united by the predicate.
T F The subject of the sentence "Man is an animal" is 'animal.'
T F The subject of the sentence "Man is not God" is 'God.'
T F Questions are not propositions.
T F "Just do it" is a proposition.
T F "All dogs go to heaven" is a proposition.
T F The three elements of any proposition are the subject, the predicate, and the copula.
T F A subject-term must have at least two words.

Carefully read "Four Basic Categorical Propositions." Review Chapter 5 if necessary.

6. Tell the quality and quantity of each proposition:

All kings are good.
No truth is simple.
Some generals are great.
Some Gauls are not brave.
All Romans are brave.
Some wars are not cruel.
All Christians are brothers.
No wars are peaceful.
Some towns are well fortified.
All truth is God's truth.
Some towns are not fortified.
Some victories are not glorious.
No tribes are safe.
All leaders are slaughtered.
Some wars are fierce.
No kings are good.

__________ **Exercises for Day 3.** **Carefully read "Contradictory and Contrary Statements." Review Chapter 6 if necessary.**

7. Indicate whether the following statements are true or false:

T F Two statements are contradictory if they differ from each other in quality but are the same in quantity.
T F The quality of the statement "All S is P" is universal.
T F The quantity of the statement "Some S is P" is particular.
T F The A statement and the O statement differ in quality and quantity.
T F The statements "All S is P" and "No S is P" can both be true at the same time.
T F The statements "All S is P" and "No S is P" can both be false at the same time.
T F The A statement and the E statement are not contradictory because, although they differ in quality, they do not differ in quantity.
T F The statement "Just do it" and the statement "All men are mortal" are contradictory.
T F The statements "All football players are big" and "No football players are big" are contrary.
T F Contrary statements cannot at the same time be false, but they can both be true.

Carefully read "Subcontrary and Subalternate Statements." Review Chapter 7 if necessary.

8. Indicate whether the following statements are true or false:

T F Two statements are subcontrary if they differ from each other in quality and are both particular.
T F The quality of the statement "All S is P" is universal.
T F The quantity of the statement "Some S is P" is particular.
T F The A statement and the I statement differ in quality and quantity.
T F The statements "All S is P" and "Some S is P" can both be true at the same time.
T F The statements "All S is P" and "Some S is P" can both be false at the same time.
T F The A statement and the E statement are not subcontrary because, although they differ in quality, they are both universal.
T F The statement "Just do it" and the statement "All men are mortal" are subcontrary.
T F The statements "All football players are big" and "Some football players are big" are subalternate.
T F Subalternate statements cannot at the same time be false, but they can both be true.

Carefully read "Distribution." Review Chapter 8 if necessary.

9. Indicate whether the following statements are true or false:

T	F	The subject-term is distributed in statements whose quantity is universal.
T	F	The subject-term is undistributed in statements whose quantity is universal.
T	F	The subject-term in the I statement is undistributed.
T	F	The subject-term in the E statement is undistributed.
T	F	In affirmative propositions, the predicate-term is always taken universally.
T	F	In negative propositions, the predicate is always taken universally.
T	F	The statement "Just do it" and the statement "All men are mortal" are subcontrary.
T	F	The statements "All football players are big" and "Some football players are big" are subalternate.
T	F	Subalternate statements cannot at the same time be false, but they can both be true.

Carefully read "Obversion, Conversion, and Contraposition." Review Chapter 9 if necessary.

10. Each of the statements on the right is logically equivalent to the statement to the left of it. Indicate whether the statement on the right is the obverse, the converse, or the contrapositive of the statement to the left of it (use *O* for obverse, *C* for converse, and *CP* for contrapositive):

All logic problems are difficult.	____	No logic problems are not difficult.
No logic problems are difficult.	____	No difficult things are logic problems.
Some logic problems are difficult.	____	Some difficult things are logic problems.
Some logic problems are not difficult.	____	Some non-difficult things are logic problems.
All logic problems are difficult.	____	All non-difficult things are not logic problems.
No logic problems are difficult.	____	No difficult things are logic problems.
Some logic problems are difficult.	____	Some logic problems are not non-difficult.
Some men are white.	____	Some white people are men.
No men are white.	____	All men are non-white.
All men are white.	____	All non-white things are not men.
Some men are not white.	____	Some non-white people are men.
Some men are white.	____	Some men are not non-white.
No men are white.	____	All men are non-white.
All men are white.	____	All non-white people are non-men.

________ Exercises for Day 4. **Carefully read "What is Deductive Inference?" Review Chapter 10 if necessary.**

11. Indicate whether the following statements are true or false:

T	F	Reasoning is the act of the mind by which we create new knowledge out of nothing.
T	F	The two kinds of reasoning are deduction and induction.
T	F	A syllogism contains three premises and a conclusion.
T	F	In a valid argument, if the premises are true, the conclusion must be true.
T	F	The minor term is the subject of the conclusion, and the major term is the predicate of the conclusion.
T	F	The major premise is the premise that contains the major term.

T F The middle term is the term that does not appear in either premise.
T F If S is identical with M, and P is identical with M, then S is identical with P.

Carefully read "Terminological Rules for Syllogisms." Review Chapter 11 if necessary.

12. Indicate whether the following statements are true or false:

T F In order for a syllogism to be valid, it must comply with all seven rules.
T F A syllogism must have a minor, major, and middle term.
T F If a syllogism commits the Fallacy of Four Terms, that means it does not contain enough terms.
T F In a valid syllogism, the minor and major term are connected together by the middle term.
T F The Fallacy of Equivocation is easier to spot than the Fallacy of Four Terms.
T F Rules I and II are considered terminological rules because they have to do with the nature of the terms in a syllogism.
T F A syllogism violates Rule II when more than one middle term appears in the premises.
T F The minor term is the subject of the conclusion.

Carefully read "Quantitative Rules for Syllogisms." Review Chapter 12 if necessary.

13. Indicate whether the following statements are true or false:

T F If a term is distributed in the conclusion, then that same term must be distributed in the premises.
T F The subject-term of an E statement is distributed.
T F Syllogisms that violate Rule IV are said to commit the Fallacy of Illicit Process.
T F The Fallacy of Illicit Major is committed when the major term is distributed in the conclusion, but not in the premises.
T F If the middle term is not distributed in either of the premises, then the syllogism is invalid.
T F The Fallacy of Undistributed Middle is committed when the middle term is distributed in the premises, but not in the conclusion.

Carefully read "Qualitative Rules for Syllogisms." Review Chapter 13 if necessary.

14. Indicate whether the following statements are true or false:

T F If there are more than three terms in a syllogism, then the syllogism violates Rule III.
T F If a syllogism has at least one affirmative premise, the conclusion must be affirmative.
T F The Fallacy of Illicit Minor occurs when the minor term is distributed in the conclusion, but not in the premises.
T F The middle term must be distributed at least once.
T F No conclusion can follow from two negative premises.
T F The minor term must be universal in both the conclusion and the premises.